BIRDS of SOUTHEASTERN MICHIGAN and SOUTHWESTERN ONTARIO

by

Alice H. Kelley

Cranbrook Institute of Science
Bloomfield Hills, Michigan

Bulletin 57

Cover: Design by Betty E. Odle
        from a photograph by Dennis F. Rupert

Map: Karen L. Rutkowski
Editor: Stella Papadakis

TABLE OF CONTENTS

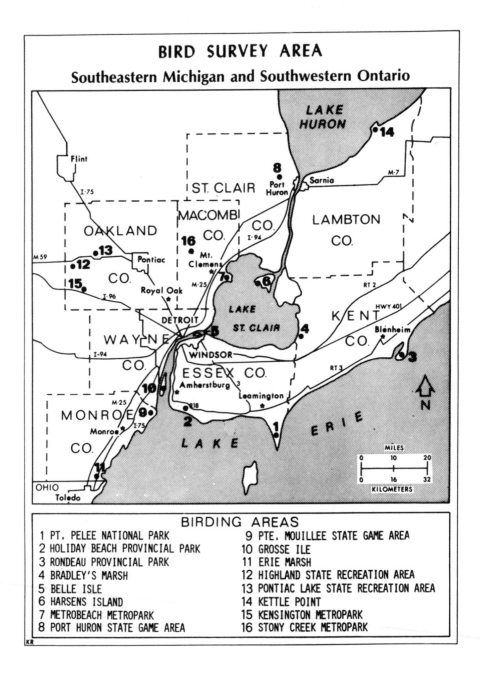

BIRD SURVEY AREA
Southeastern Michigan and Southwestern Ontario

BIRDING AREAS

1 PT. PELEE NATIONAL PARK
2 HOLIDAY BEACH PROVINCIAL PARK
3 RONDEAU PROVINCIAL PARK
4 BRADLEY'S MARSH
5 BELLE ISLE
6 HARSENS ISLAND
7 METROBEACH METROPARK
8 PORT HURON STATE GAME AREA
9 PTE. MOUILLEE STATE GAME AREA
10 GROSSE ILE
11 ERIE MARSH
12 HIGHLAND STATE RECREATION AREA
13 PONTIAC LAKE STATE RECREATION AREA
14 KETTLE POINT
15 KENSINGTON METROPARK
16 STONY CREEK METROPARK

FOREWORD

For observers interested in going beyond simple bird identification, this book is an important and helpful companion to favorite field guides. Such guides are important tools for identification, but because they cover large continental areas, the Eastern United States for example, they are of limited value in describing the status of birds of a specific locality. This book, then, supplements field guides by describing the relative abundance, migrating patterns, nesting activities, and preferred habitats of more than 300 species found within specified counties of the Erie-Huron flyway. This is a region populated by over four million people and a larger number of birds. Residents of this 6,000-square mile area of southeastern Michigan and southwestern Ontario are blessed with a great variety and abundance of bird-life because of their location on migratory routes, the position of the Great Lakes, and the character of adjacent land masses.

The author, Alice Kelley, is a graduate of the University of Wisconsin and a consultant in ornithology at Cranbrook Institute of Science. For over twenty years, observers in Michigan and Ontario have regularly reported thousands of sightings to her. As chairman of the Bird Survey Committee of the Detroit Audubon Society, she has carefully evaluated, recorded, and published summaries from this mass of data in various ornithological journals and three Cranbrook publications. Her guidance is constantly sought by amateurs and professionals alike.

Beginning as well as advanced students will find in this book a wealth of detail, facilitating keener bird observations and understanding, as well as a challenge to contribute personally to the ever-expanding record. The book reflects one of the longest and most thorough on-going records ever assembled for any region in the United States or Canada.

Robert N. Bowen
Director

PREFACE

In 1945 the Detroit Audubon Society undertook a continuing survey of the abundance, migration periods, and breeding status of birds in an eight-county area of southeastern Michigan and southwestern Ontario. One result of this was a summary, *Birds of the Detroit-Windsor Area, A Ten-Year Survey,* published in 1963 by Cranbrook Institute of Science. A second, smaller bulletin, *Changes in the Bird-Life of the Detroit-Windsor Area, 1955–1965,* updating the status of the bird-life, was published three years later. As environmental and habitat changes took place in the defined area and the amount of serious field work increased, it became obvious that an up-to-date summary was needed. Thirty years have now elapsed since the first data were gathered and reported. *Birds of Southeastern Michigan and Southwestern Ontario* summarizes the data accumulated during the thirty years (1945–1974) that the Detroit Audubon Society has sponsored the survey project.

This publication is a cooperative project, the result of careful and consistent reporting of field work by several hundred observers. It is not possible to list here the names of all who cooperated, but I acknowledge the thousands of observations which allowed me to produce this significant summary.

Cranbrook Institute of Science has maintained an interest in this continuing survey and during the years from 1945–1960 provided facilities for the committee to tabulate the data. I gratefully acknowledge the encouragement of Robert T. Hatt, former director, and the interest of Robert N. Bowen, present director, who offered to oversee the publication of this revision.

I wish to thank Joseph P. Kleiman for reading the manuscript; his suggestions were particularly valuable because of his extensive field experience. Additional comments by Dennis Rupert and Benedict C. Pinkowski regarding species of special interest to them were also helpful. I am grateful to my husband, Neil T. Kelley, for his advice and help, particularly in statistical matters, and for his patience and understanding during the preparation of the manuscript.

Alice H. Kelley

INTRODUCTION

In the years just preceding the turn of the century and for several years thereafter, many observers were well acquainted with the ornithology of southeastern Michigan and southwestern Ontario. William E. Saunders, Bradshaw H. Swales, Percy A. Taverner, Alexander W. Blain, and J. Clair Wood were prominent students of the period whose extensive field work and published accounts contributed greatly to the knowledge of the bird-life of the area. They were instrumental in organizing the Michigan Ornithological Club and the Great Lakes Ornithological Club, both of which were active until about 1910. With their passing a long period followed in which ornithological investigation in this region steadily declined and eventually became nonexistent. Except for the work of a few individuals, usually working casually and independently, the lag continued until about 1940. At that time, however, the Detroit Audubon Society and other local groups were organized which brought together people interested in birds. An interest in field work was stimulated which resulted in the Bird Survey Project, initiated in 1945 under the sponsorship of the Detroit Audubon Society.

Intensive studies of the bird-life of a specific region over an extended period of time are particularly valuable in an area undergoing rapid environmental changes. Fluctuations in populations may be evaluated and yearly variations documented; knowledge of life histories of species is increased and evidence of changes in status is more substantial. This book is a summary of such a long-term study from 1945 through 1974. It was compiled from numerical observations on all species, reported quarterly on printed forms, together with significant banding data and information on breeding birds reported on nest cards. The area of the survey has remained the same throughout the project, an eight-county region, five in southeastern Michigan and three contiguous counties in southwestern Ontario. Throughout the period of study, a quarterly summary was prepared each year for publication in *American Birds* and for the Michigan Bird Survey in the *Jack-Pine Warbler*. Unusual records were submitted to an editorial group of the Bird Survey Committee and to the Ontario Records Committee where pertinent. Nesting data were initially recorded on locally prepared nest cards, but Cornell University forms were substituted upon the start of the North American Nest Card Program, with duplicates forwarded to Cornell.

In the thirty years since record-keeping began, the Bird Survey Committee has received reports on 338 species of which 160 have been known to breed in the area. It should be mentioned that a great deal of the significant data on breeding birds was accumulated in the early years of the survey when Walter P. Nickell, Douglas S. Middleton, and their associates were extremely active in field investigation. Nesting data cards for the local area now number approximately 37,000. These are on file at Cranbrook Institute of Science as are the

1

original seasonal reports and are available for research use.

During the last fifteen years increased public interest in ecology and the environment has resulted in a growing number of concerned individuals who have developed an interest in ornithology. They have contributed to the growth and activity of the Bird Survey Project which, with other local studies, continues to document the status of birds in a metropolitan area of constant environmental change.

DESCRIPTION OF THE AREA

Position and Extent

The area studied in this survey lies between the extremes of 41°15' and 43°15' north latitude and 81°15' and 83°45' west longitude. It includes five counties in southeastern Michigan and three in southwestern Ontario separated by the St. Clair-Detroit River waterway and adjacent to lower Lake Huron and upper Lake Erie. Also included are several outlying Lake Erie islands. The land area encompasses approximately 5,916 square miles, of which 3,267 are in Michigan and 2,649 in Ontario. Lambton County is the largest in area, followed in size by Kent, Oakland, St. Clair, Essex, Wayne, Monroe, and Macomb counties.

Topography and Drainage

The land features of the region resulted from postglacial erosion during the last, Wisconsin, ice age. The Michigan portion of the region is covered by glacial detritus in varying depths. These deposits lie mainly upon rocks of Mississippian age, except in a limited portion of eastern Wayne and Monroe counties which is underlaid by limestones and sandstones of Devonian and Silurian age.

The elevations of the Michigan counties vary from less than 600 feet above sea level along the Great Lakes waterway to 1,241 feet on Pine Knob in Independence Township, Oakland County, the highest elevation in the region. The western and northwestern portions of St. Clair County, northwestern Macomb County, and much of Oakland County are covered with moderate to high moraine deposits. The eastern parts of these counties are mostly flat, representing outwash plains, till plains, and numerous features of old glacial lake beds and river deposits which extend throughout Wayne and Monroe counties to the Ohio line. Drainage by means of numerous small streams is predominantly from the higher morainic areas of the west and northwest toward the east and southeast.

Nearly all the inland lakes, estimated to be about 500, are found in Oakland County, the most rugged of the eight counties. The greatest number of inland marshes and boreal bogs are also found here. In the other Michigan counties marshes are confined to the edges of the major waterways and along streams and rivers.

The Ontario counties are generally flat or slightly rolling, except for the deeply dissected valley of the Ausable River in northern Lambton County and for a few miles of high cliffs along the Lake Erie shore in Essex and Kent counties. They are underlaid by Devonian limestones and shales which outcrop only at scattered places where they have been uncovered by river and lake erosion. There are few inland lakes or bogs and no moraines comparable in height to those of the Michigan

3

counties. However, varying thicknesses of glacial deposits cover the underlying rocks throughout.

Soils

The soils of the region are derived directly from glaciation and the subsequent leaching of original minerals and by the addition of humus generated by their vegetational cover. Coarser sand-gravel soils are found along the slopes of higher moraines, while finer clays, sandy loams, and humic soils are more common in areas with less gradient. Despite great variations, most of these soils may be characterized as acid in nature.

Vegetational Features

The present vegetation of this area moved northward in cycles, following the melting of the continental ice sheet, from regions that are now Kentucky, Tennessee, and adjacent areas. It is believed that little change in plant species has occurred during the last several hundred years. However, many species were more abundant and widely distributed about 200 years ago prior to colonization. With the rapid advance of forest clearing and marsh draining, resulting from urban expansion during the last sixty or more years, many original vegetational features have disappeared from large areas. Predominant forests today are oak-hickory, with rapidly disappearing remnants of beech-maple, mixed hardwoods, and flood-plain forest. Pine-hardwood forests are now uncommon; hemlock forests, rare. Very little virgin timber of any kind remains. Fortunately, most of the widely scattered, small stands of mature trees still remaining are publicly owned.

Large areas of swamp forest, marsh, and marginal lands have been drained or otherwise altered. In spite of current regulations, water pollution is still a problem. Cyclic shifts in water levels of the Great Lakes alter the shorelines which at present are high, resulting in a decrease in marshlands. Only the extensive marshes of the St. Clair River delta, elsewhere along Lake St. Clair, and a few other points on the Great Lakes have escaped major change, owing primarily to extensive public ownership and to private maintenance and regulation of areas belonging to private groups. These marshes may continue to be among the largest and most interesting ornithological sites of this region.

While environmental change is most obvious near centers of population, more gradual and less spectacular changes, continually taking place throughout the area, have had an effect on bird-life. Because of a lack of statistics, it is difficult to be specific about this effect other than to say it is manifested primarily in population fluctuations and distributional shifts, rather than in significant differences in composition. For example, some species of waterfowl and most birds of prey are

4

much less common today than formerly. To some extent this decrease reflects a general overall decline caused by pesticide use, rather than from changing ecological conditions. Doubtless some fringillids, and certainly the Cardinal, are more numerous now than in earlier times, apparently benefiting from an increase in suitable habitats. Several northern-type birds, prior to this survey not known to either nest or be present during nesting season, although still rare, are now recorded occasionally. On the other hand, there has been no evidence throughout the survey that species such as the Sharp-shinned Hawk and the Short-eared Owl, which once nested here occasionally, have done so since 1945.

Areas of Particular Interest

Several localities in the survey area merit special attention because of differences in topography and vegetation. The sites include either nesting habitats for several species of birds not common to the general area or geographically suitable migration points. Three of these are similar in origin and represent successions of old beach lines created when Lake Huron and Lake Erie water levels receded. Listed in order of size, they are: (1) the Ipperwash Beach area in northeastern Lambton County, bordering Lake Huron; (2) Rondeau Provincial Park, Kent County; and (3) Point Pelee National Park, Essex County.

Ipperwash Beach is made up of wind-deposited dunes, old beach lines, and extensive, fairly flat areas of sterile, sandy soils. It contains the only typical pine barrens to be found in the survey area. Growth on the old beach lines consists of birch, white cedar, and black spruce, with some jack-pine and scattered red cedar. In the low swales between the beach lines are cattails, dwarf birch, shrub willow, and coarse marsh grasses, as well as bog vegetation, including sphagnum moss and pitcher-plants. In this general area were found the only nests of the Prairie Warbler.

Rondeau Provincial Park is a blunt peninsula about six miles long from northeast to southwest and nearly three miles wide near its southwestern tip, tapering to less than half a mile at the northeast. For most of its length it consists of a series of old beaches paralleling the long axis of the peninsula, the crests of which are two or three feet higher than the depressions in which water may stand for long periods. In low places several species of trees, especially elm, ash, and red maple, attain a large size. The park contains the largest remaining stand of virgin white pine and the largest single stand of virgin beech-maple forest in the survey area. In the northern portion of the park is a long, narrow strip thickly grown with red cedar, interspersed with aromatic sumac, gray dogwood, hawthorn, and wild plum, canopied and interlaced with wild grapes. The greatest variety of habitats in the survey area is found in this park. Pileated Woodpeckers may be found during all seasons, and Prothonotary Warblers are present in the summer. In recent years Little Gulls and White-eyed Vireos have been known to nest.

Point Pelee National Park, a long peninsula tapering to a sandbar at its southern end, is world famous among ornithologists as a concentration point for large numbers of birds in both spring and fall migration. Birds in fall migration often pause at the southern terminus before flying the ten miles to Pelee Island, then, by way of other islands, to the Ohio mainland. Northbound migrants, island-hopping across Lake Erie, often congregate here in the spring in large numbers. Several rare species have been recorded only in this locality in the survey area. Land habitats are similar to those of the red cedar association of Rondeau Provincial Park except that red cedar predominates, with hackberry an important associate. Several southern elements also occur here: black walnut, honey locust, chestnut oak, and wafer ash. A shallow marsh covers several thousand acres of the east side.

Extensive marsh areas, found principally along both sides of the St. Clair-Detroit River waterway and on Strawberry, Harsens, Walpole, and Dickenson's islands, are also of particular interest. Large mainland marshes such as Bradley's Marsh, Pointe Mouillee, and the Monroe and Erie marshes, also provide suitable habitats for waterfowl and migrating shorebirds. An extensive marsh area adjoining Holiday Beach Provincial Park at the mouth of the Detroit River in Essex County also provides such habitat, but the park is best known as a vantage point for fall observation of thousands of migrating hawks, blue jays, and other birds which appear in large numbers to cross the river near this point.

An uncommon but interesting type of habitat is the boreal-type bog found locally in the northern portions of Oakland, St. Clair, and, more rarely, in Macomb counties. Fed by cold streams originating in surrounding hills, these bogs are relics of the ice age. Vegetation is characteristically northern, typical of the cold bogs found farther north. Certain such habitats exhibit an overlapping in the breeding ranges of several summering species.

In the survey area are also many other interesting habitats which are included in public lands and not then subject to encroaching urbanization. Thousands of acres are included in state recreation and game areas and in the parks of the Huron-Clinton Metropolitan Authority.

Many of the ecologically interesting wildlife areas mentioned above represent public lands which were preserved by the farsightedness of federal, state, and local planners. Because of their proximity to large metropolitan areas, they are accessible for present and future use and enjoyment by a great many grateful people.

PLACE NAMES

Belle Isle, Wayne County
Bloomfield Township, Oakland County
Bradley's Marsh, Kent County
Cranbrook campus, Oakland County
Detroit, Wayne County
Dover Marsh, Kent County
Erie Marsh, Monroe County
Grosse Ile, Wayne County
Harsens Island, St. Clair County
Highland Recreation Area, Oakland County
Holiday Beach Provincial Park, Essex County
Ipperwash Beach, Lambton County
Kensington Metropark, Oakland County
Kettle Point, Lambton County
Lake Orion, Oakland County
Metrobeach Metropark, Macomb County
Mt. Clemens, Macomb County
Pontiac Lake, Oakland County
Proud Lake, Oakland County
Port Huron, St. Clair County
Port Huron Game Area, St. Clair County
Pte. Mouillee, Monroe County
Pt. Pelee, Essex County
Rondeau Provincial Park, Kent County
St. Luke's Club, Kent County
Sarnia Bay, Lambton County
Stony Creek Metropark, Oakland and Macomb counties
Wheatley, Essex County

SPECIES ACCOUNTS

The field work of the survey period, 1945–1974, produced data on 337 species, including three hybrids. This number represents an increase of 52 species since the publication of the ten-year survey twenty years ago. No attempt has been made to deal with the subspecies or other hybrids. One additional species recorded in early 1975 before this publication went to press is included because of its special significance. This brings the total to 338 species as listed in the following accounts.

A general statement regarding abundance and status is given for each species, based on quantitative data regularly reported. Such terminology does not represent rigid concepts, but serves as a guide of relative value. Terms used to indicate relative abundance are as follows:

Abundant: Species occurs in very large numbers in suitable habitats, often congregating in large flocks;

Common: Species occurs regularly throughout the area in frequent observations of fairly large numbers;

Fairly Common: Species found in moderate numbers, less frequently reported;

Uncommon: Species occurs regularly in suitable habitat, but in small numbers and with comparatively few occurrences;

Rare: Species may be recorded only a few times each year or less often in very small numbers;

Accidental: Species occurs well beyond usual range, generally recorded only once or twice.

Spring and fall migration periods are based on long-time averages. To allow for yearly variation in migration, average or normal periods are given as "early" in the month (first ten days), "mid-month" (11th through 20th), and "late" (21st through last day of month). Extreme early and late dates may be considered as unusual records.

Nesting data for breeding birds are included in a second paragraph of the species account. Nesting seasons are indicated by general and specific dates similar to those for migration periods and use the same terminology. Extreme nesting dates represent the earliest and latest dates of breeding activity reported for each species; a statement of the status on that date is also given. As previously mentioned, many of the extreme dates were established during the the first fifteen years of the survey because of extensive individual investigation of various species at that time.

Nomenclature and taxonomic arrangement follow the *American Ornithologists' Union Check-List of North American Birds* (Fifth Edition, 1957) and later changes authorized in the *Thirty-second Supplement to the American Ornithologists' Union Check-List of North American Birds* (Auk 90: 411–419, April 1973). All common names follow the fifth edition and most of the changes in the supplement. The abbreviated form UMMZ, indicating location of specimens, refers to the University of Michigan Museum of Zoology.

Because Point Pelee National Park is a well-known concentration point for birds, records tend to be somewhat distorted by the large number of observers as well as birds. Maximum numbers for several species were recorded at Pt. Pelee because of its geographic position and cannot be regarded as representative of general abundance throughout the area. In spite of some inequities in field coverage and distortion due to location, the following species accounts represent a serious attempt to present a comprehensive summary of the bird-life for the past thirty years.

Family GAVIIDAE. Loons

Common Loon   *Gavia immer*

Regular migrant. Spring migration usually evident during last week in March (earliest: March 21, 1952), increasing to peak in mid-April. Most have moved north by the third week of May. Fall migration most evident from early October through November; two September records (earliest: September 5, 1954), eleven December records, and one on January 30, 1952. Sometimes numerous along Lake Huron in Lambton County, maximum of 2,000 at Ipperwash Beach on November 21, 1971, and 1,380 at Kettle Point on October 26, 1973.

One breeding record. Two adults with one half-grown young were found at Lonesome Lake, northern Oakland County, on July 23, 1952 (Daubendiek and others), also the site of an earlier but unconfirmed nesting record. There are nine other summer sight records.

Arctic Loon   *Gavia arctica*

Accidental. One record. A bird was observed at Kettle Point October 28 to 31, 1973 (Rider and Rupert); seen with Common Loons (*G. immer*). A second bird was reported at Pt. Pelee on December 17, 1974 (Morin).

Red-throated Loon   *Gavia stellata*

Uncommon migrant. Except for one record from Harsens Island, all were from Canadian counties, mainly Rondeau, Ipperwash Beach, Kettle Point, and Pt. Pelee. Reports increased after 1965 with a maximum of forty-one birds in the fall of 1973. Reported in the spring from April 23 throughout May and in the fall through late November. One summer record on August 2, 1952, and one in winter on December 24, 1971.

Family PODICIPEDIDAE. Grebes

Red-necked Grebe *Podiceps grisegena*

Uncommon migrant. Reported six times in spring, more often in fall (maximum of sixty-three birds at Ipperwash Beach on October 11, 1973). Three winter records: a bird found inland in Macomb County on February 3, 1959, which later died; another on a snow-covered beach at Pt. Pelee on December 16, 1951; and two birds on the St. Clair River on February 24, 1968.

Horned Grebe *Podiceps auritus*

Fairly common migrant. Spring migration begins in mid-March, continuing uniformly throughout April and first three weeks in May (latest: May 28, 1950). One summer record at Proud Lake on August 11, 1950. Fall migrants return in mid-September (earliest: September 13, 1953) and remain in good numbers throughout November (maximum of 500 at Pt. Pelee on November 6, 1966). Scattered winter reports; from thirty to fifty birds in three winters.

Eared Grebe *Podiceps nigricollis*

Rare migrant. First recorded at Ipperwash Beach on April 26 to 29, 1969 (Rupert). Since this first sighting, single birds have been reported each year, twice in spring, as follows: November 15, 1970, Sarnia Bay; April 27, 1971, and October 25, 1972, Rondeau; November 25, 1973, Sarnia Bay; May 6, 1974, Wheatley; and October 28 to 29, 1974, Pt. Pelee.

Western Grebe *Aechmophorus occidentalis*

Accidental. A single record. A bird was observed at Pt. Pelee in bright sunlight close inshore on October 25, 1949 (Reynolds).

Pied-billed Grebe *Podilymbus podiceps*

Common migrant and summer resident. Migration evident by mid-March, heaviest throughout April and first two weeks in May. Abundant in fall migration from mid-September throughout October, less numerous in November; scattered reports in winter.

Breeds regularly in deeper marshes along both major waterways and inland lakes; records for all counties except Lambton. Nesting usually begins by last week in May (earliest: May 19, 1951, two nests with six and seven eggs, St. Luke's Club) and extends well into mid-summer. Nests are placed on floating, anchored mats. Early dates for young: May 24 and 26, 1974, Metrobeach. Young of the year, still

10

attended by adults, reported five times in September (latest: September 24, 1967, Erie Marsh).

Family PELECANIDAE. Pelicans

White Pelican   *Pelecanus erythrorhynchos*

Rare visitant. In 1946 three birds remained at Erie Marsh from August 12 to September 15 (Campbell collected one). Two reports in 1947: seven birds at Pte. Mouillee on May 11 and two birds at Erie Marsh from August 30 through September. In 1948 three birds remained at Pte. Mouillee from August 13 through October 9. One report from Pt. Pelee of two birds on September 24, 1964.

Family SULIDAE. Gannets and Boobies

Gannet   *Morus bassanus*

One record of this oceanic species. A bird was seen at Pt. Pelee on November 25, 1973 (Kleiman, Greenhouse, and Wilson).

Family PHALACROCORACIDAE. Cormorants

Double-crested Cormorant   *Phalacrocorax auritus*

Fairly common migrant; rare summer resident. Migration noted from early April (earliest: March 26, 1949) through May, with birds present in summer at Pt. Pelee from 1948 to 1954 and one bird at Pte. Mouillee on June 14, 1973. Fall migration evident near mid-September; most reports from Pt. Pelee. Numbers greatly reduced within the last ten years, but with slight indication of recent increase (twenty-seven birds in Essex County in 1971). Eight December records (latest: December 26, 1973).

Known to breed only on the Chicken Islands, a group of small reefs in the Ontario waters of Lake Erie, a few miles west of Pelee Island. A small colony has nested with varying success on at least one of these islands since about 1939. Thirteen nests were reported there on May 22, 1954 (Langlois), one new but empty, the rest with eggs (one still with young on July 2).

Family ARDEIDAE. Herons and Bitterns

Great Blue Heron   *Ardea herodias*

Common local resident, recently less numerous. Spring migrants arrive about mid-March and are common soon thereafter. Reported regularly through October, with numbers diminishing in November and early December. Found in winter in Great Lakes marshes (maximum of ninety at Erie Marsh in winter of 1971–72).

Breeds regularly, recently somewhat reduced because of lack of suitable habitat and human interference. Although largest concentrations are now found on Lake Erie islands in mixed colonies, at least three large inland colonies of up to ninety nests were active through 1974. Rookeries may be occupied as early as mid-March, but nesting proper usually begins about two weeks later (earliest: March 24, 1952). Nests are almost invariably placed in tops of tall trees, often several in same tree. Latest: July 22, 1972, nest with one young, Proud Lake.

Green Heron   *Butorides virescens*

Fairly common resident. Average arrival about third week in April (earliest: April 16, 1964). After nesting season (late July through September) birds gather in small groups; numbers diminish rapidly during first two weeks in October (latest: October 24, 1972).

Breeds regularly, but in reduced numbers in recent years; generally distributed. Nesting usually begins in last half of May (earliest: May 5, 1968, nest with eggs); interruptions may extend season to late July. Nests are places in trees or low shrubs, usually near water. Normally the species is non-colonial, but in 1972 Radcliffe studied a very large colony of forty pairs at Drayton Plains Nature Center, Oakland County. Nests were placed in low willows; three nests contained eggs as late as August 27.

Little Blue Heron   *Florida caerulea*

Uncommon visitant. Four birds recorded in May; post-breeding birds recorded from July 11 through early October. Largest number (fifty-eight birds) was seen in 1949 at four stations; scarce since 1969.

Cattle Egret   *Bubulcus ibis*

Since this African species was recorded in Florida in 1941, it has rapidly expanded its range. First recorded in local area at Erie Marsh in 1961 and in Dover Marsh the following year. Reported each year since except 1968 (maximum of twenty-seven in spring of 1973 in Essex and Monroe counties). Only two records from inland locations. In the summer of 1974, the species was found to nest on Pelee Island, Essex County (Campbell).

Great Egret   *Casmerodius albus*

Fairly common post-breeding visitant; uncommon and local breeder. Reported more frequently in spring after 1964 (earliest: March

7, 1973; three other March records). Most numerous from late July to early October (maximum of 200 at Pte. Mouillee in late August 1974), with a few remaining until early November (latest: November 9, 1954).

Current breeding abundance and distribution not clear; known to be breeding currently on Stoney Island in the Detroit River and on the islands in Lake Erie, including Pelee Island (1974). Earlier breeding records show three locations: May 10, 1953, an occupied nest on East Sister Island, Lake Erie; April 18 through 24, 1953, nine active nests on Stoney Island, Detroit River; May 1954, seven active nests on Dickinson Island, Lake St. Clair. In all instances, birds were nesting in long-established mixed colonies.

Snowy Egret   *Egretta thula*

Rare visitor. Recorded nine times from 1947 through 1974; most reports were in 1970 when two birds were seen at Rondeau on May 6 and two at Bradley's Marsh on September 5. Reports of single birds from Erie Marsh (three records), Pt. Pelee, Bradley's Marsh, and Rondeau in April, May, August, and September.

Louisiana Heron   *Hydranassa tricolor*

Rare visitor. First recorded at Rondeau on May 18, 1957, and again on May 1, 1959 (Ussher and Goodwill). Two records from Erie Shooting Club, Monroe County; one from May 8 to 20, 1965 (Black and Tordoff) and another on May 27, 1967 (Kleiman). Recent records more numerous: June 1, 1969, one bird at Bradley's Marsh; May 14, 1970, two birds, and May 22, 1971, one bird, Rondeau; September 1, 1974, two birds at Erie Marsh, the only fall record.

Black-crowned Night Heron   *Nycticorax nycticorax*

Summer resident, formerly common but less so in recent years. Spring migrants arrive in March, not common until mid-May. Numbers begin to diminish in mid-October until end of month; several November and December records. There have been reports of birds wintering, but none in recent years.

Has nested in five survey counties, but fluctuating water levels and other factors have caused abandonment of previous sites; current status not clear. Known to breed on Stoney Island in the Detroit River and probably at Walpole Island, Kent County, and the marshes on the eastern side of Lake St. Clair. Rookeries may be occupied by late March; full clutches of three or four eggs not usually completed until about a month later. Extreme dates: March 24, 1945, thirty nests at Stoney Island; July 15, 1951, four active nests at Bradley's Marsh.

Yellow-crowned Night Heron   *Nyctanassa violacea*

Rare visitant and summer resident. Expansion of range of this species evident; first recorded in survey area in 1964: from April 13 to 15, a bird at Wheatley (Chesterfield and Botham), and from September 22 to October 1, one at Holiday Beach (Thompson). On May 8, 1965 one was found at Erie Marsh. Reported in 1970 at the Cranbrook campus (Radcliffe) and on June 28 at Erie Marsh (Kleiman); on April 28, 1974 one was photographed on Pelee Island (Pratt).

On May 30, 1971 a pair was found nesting (two young raised) near the Rouge River, Wayne County (Fisher); the same year a pair raised one young in Monroe County (Greenhouse). An unsuccessful nesting was attempted in Monroe County again in 1972.

Least Bittern   *Ixobrychus exilis*

Fairly common summer resident. Migrants normally arrive in early May (earliest: April 27, 1952). Fall migration evident during last two weeks of September (latest: October 10, 1954, Bradley's Marsh).

Breeds regularly in deep water marshes. Nesting usually begins in early June (earliest: May 19, 1946, nest with eggs, Pte. Mouillee) and reaches a peak, with renestings, late that month or early July, with some young in nests into August (latest: August 19, 1952, active nest, Otter Lake, Oakland County). Concentrations in local areas suggest semicolonial nesting.

American Bittern   *Botaurus lentiginosus*

Fairly common summer resident. Early spring migrants reported from March 25 through April 10, with one recorded on March 1, 1952. Gradual withdrawal in October; two November records, four December, and two in January.

Breeds in moderate numbers throughout the area, but somewhat reduced in recent years. Nesting begins by last half of May (earliest: May 12, 1948, two nests with five eggs each only fifty-eight feet apart, Warren, Macomb County) and sometimes extends into July (latest: July 26, 1952, adults with one young of year, Lake Orion).

Family THRESKIORNITHADAE. Ibises

Glossy Ibis   *Plegadis* (sp.)

Uncommon visitant. Two birds reported before 1967: May 22, 1954, and May 18 through 22, 1960, both in the Ontario marshes of Lake St. Clair, Kent County. In 1967 single birds were observed on April 24 at Erie Marsh, on May 20 at Pt. Pelee, and on May 21 at Bradley's Marsh. From 1968 through 1971 a total of thirty-two birds was recorded at Rondeau and Harsens Island, as well as the above-mentioned marshes, in both spring and fall; maximum of eighteen from May 4 through 10, 1971, at Bradley's Marsh.

White Ibis *Eudocimus albus*

Accidental. One was present from September 19 through 26, 1970, at Harsens Island (photographed by Wells). One was also observed at Pt. Pelee on September 27, 1970 (Van Vliet and others). (6353)

Family ANATIDAE. Swans, Geese, and Ducks

Mute Swan *Cygnus olor*

Introduced. Five reports of one or two birds at Erie Marsh and Pte. Mouillee in 1945, 1946, and 1949; none until 1968, more numerous thereafter. Reported in some numbers (up to twenty-seven), mostly in Oakland, Kent, Lambton, and Essex counties. A pair nested at Bradley's Marsh in 1969, with five cygnets on May 25. Nested success-fully also in Oakland County at inland lakes near Pontiac in 1972, 1973, and 1974.

Whistling Swan *Olor columbianus*

Common migrant, abundant in spring. Large numbers stop off on northward migration, particularly in Lake St. Clair in the vicinity of Wallaceburg, Kent County (18,500 in 1973; 23,000 in 1974; both in late March). Most have left by mid-May. Three summer records at Pte. Mouillee. Fall migration begins about mid-October, heaviest in November; winters regularly in small numbers.

Canada Goose *Branta canadensis*

Abundant migrant; locally common summer resident. Spring migration heavy through March and April and into early May.

Breeds regularly in Oakland County, but also recorded in smaller numbers in Kent and Macomb counties. Extreme dates: April 17, 1954, two nests with six and eight eggs, Kent Lake, Oakland County; June 20, 1952, an adult with several young, Pontiac Lake, Oakland County.

Abundant in fall migration during October and November; large concentrations at Jack Miner's Bird Sanctuary near Kingsville, Essex County. Found in considerable numbers (maximum of 12,400) there in winter.

Brant *Branta bernicla*

Uncommon migrant. Recorded regularly since 1966 in fall from late October through November. Two records from Pt. Pelee, remainder from the Lake Huron shore in Lambton County; maximum of 180 on October 23, 1971, at Ipperwash Beach.

White-fronted Goose   *Anser albifrons*

Accidental. First reported at Kensington Metropark on December 3 and 4, 1967. Two later records from Jack Miner's Bird Sanctuary, Kingsville, Essex County: one on October 11, 1970, and one from March 20 through 28, 1971.

Snow Goose   *Chen caerulescens*

Uncommon migrant, less numerous in spring. Both color phases occur, with the blue phase birds considerably more numerous. Recorded from March 7 to May 27 in spring. Fall migration evident from mid-October throughout November; two December records (latest: December 11, 1953).

Fulvous Tree Duck   *Dendrocygna bicolor*

Accidental. Three shot by hunters at North Cape, Monroe County, on October 14, 1962 (specimen UMMZ). Two birds present for two weeks in June 1974 at an inland pond in Bloomfield Township, Oakland County.

Mallard   *Anas platyrhynchos*

Common migrant and summer resident. Spring migration heavy from late March through May. Most numerous in fall, with large numbers present through November in Lake St. Clair, lower Detroit River, and western Lake Erie (maximum of 11,500 counted in aerial survey on November 23, 1948). Many remain throughout winter.

Breeds commonly in all counties. One instance of semicolonial nesting behavior, perhaps by feral birds, noted on Belle Isle in mid-July 1957: ten nests with eggs in a small area, some only six feet apart. Earliest nesting: March 26, 1971, nest with eggs; latest: October 9, 1966, nine young hatched (extremely late).

Black Duck   *Anas rubripes*

Common summer resident and migrant. Spring migration from mid-March through May. Abundant in fall, with large numbers often present in winter.

Breeds regularly, but in lesser numbers than the Mallard (*A. platyrhunchos*); somewhat reduced in recent years. Earliest date: April 9, 1952, nest with two eggs; latest: July 28, 1952, adult with six young, Plymouth, Wayne County.

16

Gadwall   *Anas strepera*

Regular migrant. Recorded in generally small numbers (maximum of 155 in Monroe County on April 14, 1968) in spring from early February through May. Nine reports of one or two birds in June and July. Fall migration evident from mid-August through November; three December records. Since 1970 one or two birds have wintered at Belle Isle and in the St. Clair River.

Pintail   *Anas acuta*

Common migrant; rare summer resident. Migration begins in early March, heaviest from March 20 to April 20. Two June records, three July records, and two early August records probably represent summering stragglers; four present throughout the summer in 1970 at Rondeau. Fall migration evident from late August through November; reduced numbers in December. A few birds have wintered at Grosse Ile, Belle Isle, Erie Marsh, and the St. Clair River.

Six breeding records from private duck marshes in Kent County. At St. Luke's Club: May 20, 1951, nest with nine eggs; May 10, 1973, seven eggs; May 22, 1954, female with five young. At Dover Marsh: May 22, 1954, female with five young. At Bradley's Marsh: June 12, 1959, female with eight half-grown young; May 27, 1966, nest with nine eggs. One breeding record from Monroe County in 1967.

Green-winged Teal   *Anas crecca*

Fairly common migrant; rare summer resident. Scarce before mid-March, with migration through first half of May; maximum of 375 in spring on April 3 at Pte. Mouillee. Migrants more numerous in fall than spring, appearing in mid-August; most numerous in November. Five winter records, including 33 birds at Ipperwash Beach on December 26, 1970. In 1971 a male of the Old World sub-species Eurasian Teal was observed at Pt. Pelee from March 27 through 30 (Greenhouse, Kleiman, and Ryff).

One breeding record of an adult with five young at Rondeau on July 21, 1970. Several birds reported in summer at Rondeau and at Erie Marsh from 1965 through 1970 but without breeding evidence.

Blue-winged Teal   *Anas discors*

Common migrant and summer resident. Spring migrants generally appear in late March (earliest: March 13, 1953 and 1966); most recorded from early April to mid-May. Summer residents augmented by migrants in late August; most numerous in September. Numbers decrease gradually in October and November. Two December records (latest: December 29, 1951).

Breeds commonly. Nests with normal clutches of nine to twelve

17

eggs found by mid-May (earliest: May 1, 1969, nest with eggs, Pt. Pelee) but majority reported in late May through June with scattered reports for July; one record of an adult with thirteen half-grown young on August 12, 1950. Several nests reported with one or more eggs of Ring-necked Pheasant (*Phasianus colchicus*) in addition to those of host. Nests were found in Common Tern (*Sterna hirundo*) colony at Metrobeach.

European Wigeon   *Anas penelope*

Rare straggler, more frequent since 1960. Reported fourteen times in spring from Erie Marsh, Kettle Point, Pt. Pelee, Bradley's Marsh, and Sarnia Bay (three different birds in 1972). Reported in fall and winter at Rondeau on November 11 and December 30, 1967; at Belle Isle on November 28, 1970.

American Wigeon   *Anas americana*

Common migrant; rare summer resident. Spring migration begins in early March, heaviest from late March to mid-May. Fall migrants scarce before mid-August, then present all fall through December; winters regularly on Belle Isle (from five to twenty birds reported).

Two breeding records. On July 31, 1958, a female with five young found in the Raisin River marshes just east of Monroe, Monroe County (one young captured, died in captivity, specimen UMMZ). On July 5, 1967, adults with seven young found at Kensington Metropark where they remained as a family group until August 13. Five other July records.

Northern Shoveler   *Anas clypeata*

Fairly common migrant; rare summer resident. Spring migration begins in mid-March, usually over by mid-May. Regularly reported in fall after September 15 until end of November. Six winter records.

Four breeding records, all from Kent County. Recorded as follows: at Mud Creek Marsh on June 24, 1951, female with seven downy young; at St. Luke's Club on June 22, 1953, female with two young; at Bradley's Marsh in mid-July 1954, female with two young; at Dover Marsh on May 28, 1966, nest with seven eggs. Six summer records of single birds in July and August.

Wood Duck   *Aix sponsa*

Fairly common migrant and summer resident. Normally arrives during last half of March, most numerous from mid-April to mid-May. Often fairly numerous in late summer and fall, particularly at Pt. Pelee (maximum of 300). Gradual withdrawal noted in October and November, with scattered winter records.

Breeds regularly but locally in varying numbers. Normal clutches of eight to eleven eggs reported each month from April through August (earliest: April 25, 1948, nest with eleven eggs, Birmingham, Oakland County; April 29, 1974, young hatching, Stony Creek Metropark). Summer nests doubtless are because of failure of first attempts (latest: August 15, 1972, female with six well-grown young, Bloomfield Hills, Oakland County). Sites ranged from nesting boxes at low elevations to one in a cavity in an oak (*Quercus,* sp.) sixty feet above the ground where young were observed leaving the nest.

Redhead   *Aythya americana*

Abundant migrant, less numerous in recent years; rare summer resident. Apparently was previously a regular breeder at St. Anne's and Walpole islands in the St. Clair River delta and in the mouth of the Johnstone Channel, Kent County, but no broods or nests reported since 1954. However, birds have been recorded in summer at Big Creek (Essex County), Pt. Pelee, Sarnia Bay, Bradley's Marsh, and Erie Marsh. Fall migration begins in early October and continues throughout the fall, with good numbers remaining through the winter in Lake St. Clair and western Lake Erie. In recent years reported in smaller numbers than the 8,500 counted in an aerial census in February 1950.

Ring-necked Duck   *Aythya collaris*

Fairly common migrant. Spring migration extends from mid-March through mid-May (latest: May 20, 1949); most reported from inland lakes in small numbers up to 50. Fall migration begins in late September (earliest: September 20, 1945) continuing through November; maximum of 2,000 at Kensington Metropark in November 1968. Scattered winter reports, mainly from Grosse Ile, Belle Isle, and the St. Clair River.

Canvasback   *Aythya valisineria*

Abundant migrant and winter visitant. Winters in large numbers in Lake St. Clair and lower Detroit River; somewhat reduced in recent years. Numbers diminish through April, with most gone by mid-May. Scattered summer records through 1972, mainly single birds at Pte. Mouillee and Lake St. Clair. Fall migrants arrive in early October and are abundant by the end of the month.

Greater Scaup   *Aythya marila*

Fairly common migrant and winter visitant. Because of difficulty in distinguishing this species from Lesser Scaup (*A. affinis*), the majority of records were submitted as *Scaup* (sp.). Records citing species indicate that the present species (*A. marila*) is the least numerous.

Flocks begin to arrive in late September or early October and remain in large numbers throughout the winter in Lake St. Clair, the Detroit River, and western Lake Erie. Most numerous in March and April, decreasing until the end of migration in mid-May.

Lesser Scaup   *Aythya affinis*

Common migrant and winter visitant. Most numerous in fall and spring; present in large numbers in winter. Occasional summer reports of birds identified as this species from Pte. Mouillee, Ipperwash Beach, Metrobeach, and two inland lakes in Oakland County.

Common Goldeneye   *Bucephala clangula*

Abundant migrant and winter visitant. Most numerous in winter, with numbers diminishing from late April through mid-May. Reported in summer in 1953 (two birds on June 3 on St. Clair River and five on July 8 at Pt. Pelee) and in 1968 (one bird on July 6 at Erie Marsh). Scattered fall reports from late September (earliest: September 27, 1949) to early November when numbers increase greatly.

Barrow's Goldeneye   *Bucephala islandica*

Accidental. First recorded at Grosse Ile on December 31, 1960 (Valentine). Since then single birds have been observed at Sarnia Bay and the Canadian side of the St. Clair River as follows: December 14, 1966, December 30, 1967, February 14 through March 1, 1970, and January 22 through March 1, 1972 (Rupert and others). Two birds were seen on Lake Huron, Lambton County, on December 31, 1967, and one at Wheatley on April 10, 1971.

Bufflehead   *Bucephala albeola*

Fairly common migrant and winter visitant. Present in winter, usually in flocks smaller than 100, with added migrants in March and April; most gone by mid-May. Four July records from Rondeau, Ipperwash Beach, and Erie Marsh. Fall migration evident by mid-October, heaviest in November.

Oldsquaw   *Clangula hyemalis*

Uncommon migrant. Reported in fall from the earliest date of October 21; most numerous in late fall and winter with a maximum of 275 on November 4, 1967, on Lake Huron at Pinery Park, Lambton County. Most have gone by the end of April. Seven May reports (latest: May 29, 1968). Most reported from Lake Huron, St. Clair River, and the Detroit River at Belle Isle.

Harlequin Duck *Histrionicus histrionicus*

Rare visitant. First survey and state record was an immature male seen on the St. Clair River near the Blue Water Bridge, St. Clair County (Barker), then collected (UMMZ) on February 7, 1962. Later records as follows: March 16, 1969, a male on the Detroit River at Windsor (Kidd); December 20, 1970, Grosse Ile (Greenhouse and Kleiman); December 28, 1971, two birds at Kettle Point (Rupert); November 18, 1973, Sarnia Bay (Rupert); November 23, 1973, two birds at Port Franks, Lambton County (Rider, Kleiman, and Greenhouse).

Common Eider *Somateria mollissima*

Accidental. Single birds reported twice in Sarnia Bay: November 13, 1966 (Rupert) and November 20, 1967 (Rupert and Lamb). One also observed offshore at Pt. Pelee on November 24, 1968 (Kleiman).

King Eider *Somateria spectabilis*

Rare visitant. Two reports of birds shot: November 16, 1950, Mitchell's Bay, Lake St. Clair, Kent County, and October 30, 1966, two at Erie Marsh. Sight records of single birds as follows: December 24, 1970, offshore at Wheatley (Kleiman and Greenhouse); March 5, 1972, St. Clair River at Sombra, Lambton County (Rupert and Wilson); November 30, 1973, Kettle Point (photographed by Rider).

Two other eiders were reported without species identification: one on the lower Detroit River on January 16, 1971 (Kleiman) and the second at Pt. Pelee from May 2 through 9, 1971.

White-winged Scoter *Melanitta deglandi*

Fairly common migrant. Few reported in fall (earliest: October 10, 1949 and 1953). Occasional fairly large flocks in winter (maximum of 200) and spring (maximum of 200, May 13, 1965, Wheatley; and 60 on May 8, 1954, Pt. Pelee). One summer record on June 10, 1952, at Ipperwash Beach.

Surf Scoter *Melanitta perspicillata*

Uncommon migrant. Most reports in fall from mid-October through early-December; one winter report on February 8, 1968, Lambton County. Most numerous along Lake Huron shore, Lambton County, (maximum of 22 birds) where season total for fall of 1971 was 188 birds and for fall of 1973, 98 birds. Five spring records of one to six birds, mostly from Pt. Pelee.

Black Scoter *Melanitta nigra*

Fairly common migrant. Most reported in fall, usually in flocks of less than 50, from early October through November; three December records. Numerous in fall of 1972 when flocks of up to 350 were counted at Kettle Point. One or two birds reported four times in spring from late April through mid-May.

Ruddy Duck *Oxyura jamaicensis*

Common migrant; rare summer resident. Spring migration begins about mid-March and continues through the first two weeks of May. Occasionally occurs in large numbers in April (up to 2,000) in the Monroe County marshes and lower Detroit River. Six recent summer records without breeding evidence. Fall migration begins in late September and continues through early November; scattered winter records of very small numbers.

Thirteen breeding records, all from immediate vicinity of Walpole Island, Kent County, from 1949 through 1954; maximum of nine nests in 1954. None since.

Hooded Merganser *Lophodytes cucullatus*

Fairly common migrant, most numerous in fall; rare summer resident. Spring migration is most evident in March through mid-April. Fall migration begins in September but remains light through October, increasing in November and early December; found on inland lakes as well as the Great Lakes. Uniformly reported throughout winter.

Two pair nested in Wood Duck (*Aix sponsa*) houses in Holly Township, Oakland County, in 1969; nests found with eggs in May (Eldon and Lenz). A few sight records in August.

A hybrid between this species and Common Goldeneye (*Bucephala clangula*) was present in the St. Clair River near Sombra, Lambton County, in the winter of 1968 (Rupert); evidently the same bird returned for the following six years. A second hybrid bird was present in 1973.

Common Merganser *Mergus merganser*

Very common migrant; rare summer resident. Fall migrants recorded by September 8, becoming numerous in early November. Abundant in winter (several reports of 2,000 to 4,000 birds at Pt. Pelee) and in spring until May. Three summer sight records.

Three breeding records of females with downy young at Kettle Point in 1950 and 1951; none since.

Red-breasted Merganser *Mergus serrator*

Abundant migrant. Especially numerous in spring through mid-May (flocks up to 10,000), decreasing until end of month. Scattered summer records from Pt. Pelee, Pte. Mouillee, and lower Detroit River. Fall migration, which begins in late September, is heaviest in November; birds reported in good numbers (up to 1,000) throughout winter.

Family CATHARTIDAE. American Vultures

Turkey Vulture   *Cathartes aura*

Fairly common migrant; uncommon breeder. Migrants appear near mid-March (one early record, March 1, 1953); reported singly or in small groups. Fall migration heaviest from mid-September through early October. Few reports of more than 50 birds except during fall hawk-watch (1,128 birds counted at Holiday Beach in fall of 1974).

Reported uniformly throughout summer; less numerous since 1965. Although the species may currently nest in small numbers, only one nesting has been reported (adults with two young on May 25, 1974, Oakland County). Three early records from Kent County in 1949, 1952, and 1954.

Family ACCIPITRIDAE. Hawks and Harriers

Goshawk   *Accipiter gentilis*

Uncommon migrant and winter visitant. Reported more frequently after 1965; particularly numerous in fall of "flight year" 1973 when thirty-one birds were recorded, most at Pt. Pelee.

Sharp-shinned Hawk   *Accipiter striatus*

Regular migrant, numerous in fall. Uncommon in spring, reported from mid-March through May. Recorded several times in late June in Lambton County, once in Oakland County. Early fall migrants appear in late August (earliest: August 15, 1952); migration heavy from mid-September through October, gradually decreasing through mid-November; scattered winter records mostly from Kent and Lambton counties. Large numbers concentrate at Pt. Pelee (up to 1,000) to move across Lake Erie as well as at Holiday Beach (total of 5,900 counted in 1974) to cross at the mouth of the Detroit River.

Cooper's Hawk   *Accipiter cooperii*

Fairly common resident before 1965, scarce thereafter. Some evidence of spring migration by mid-April. In fall migrants are present from mid-September through mid-October, most reported from Holiday Beach and Pt. Pelee. Numbers reduced in recent years: no large flights comparable to the forty or more reported in the 1950s; eighty-eight counted in fall of 1974 when observers were present at Holiday Beach for twenty-seven days.

Previously nested regularly in at least four counties, but in recent years nesting reported only at Kensington Metropark and Stony Creek Metropark. Birds have been present at Stony Creek some seasons when not known to nest. The small number of nest reports show an early date of April 10, 1953 (adult repairing a nest) and a late date of May 21, 1958 (nest with four eggs).

Red-tailed Hawk   *Buteo jamaicensis*

Fairly common resident and migrant. Increased numbers move into area in winter, particularly in St. Clair and Macomb counties. Spring migration evident in April and May, with breeding birds remaining. Fall migration especially notable at Pt. Pelee and Holiday Beach, the flight lanes across Lake Erie and the lower Detroit River. Migration heaviest in October and November, with good-sized groups recorded as late as mid-December (thirty on December 15, 1968).

Breeds regularly, but not verified in all counties. Evidently suffered less reduction in recent years than other species of hawks. Nesting begins early, usually by last week in March (earliest: March 13, 1969, adult incubating); young normally leave nest by end of June (latest: July 7, 1946, one young out of nest).

Red-shouldered Hawk   *Buteo lineatus*

Resident, previously fairly common, scarce in recent years; regular migrant. Reported in winter through spring, with only a few spring flights noted. Fall migration similar to that of previous species (*B. jamaicensis*), but in much smaller numbers (88 in fall of 1973; 116 in 1974); lowest numbers from 1964 through 1968 with slight increase thereafter.

Previously bred regularly, but practically absent since 1960; regularly reported nesting only in vicinity of Stony Creek Metropark (two successful nests with three young fledged in 1974). Nesting data from previous years indicate that nesting usually begins by first week in April, often at nest site of previous seasons (earliest: April 30, 1949, four eggs); young have fledged by early July.

Broad-winged Hawk   *Buteo platypterus*

Abundant fall migrant; rare resident. Spring migrants appear in early April, usually in small groups of ten to thirty. Since 1951 cooperative studies of fall hawk migration have produced data on numbers, species flight lanes, and weather conditions, particularly in reference to this species. A migration route is followed which roughly parallels the north shore of Lake Erie; approaching local counties, the route usually takes a southwesterly direction across the Detroit River near its mouth. Holiday Beach has proved a good vantage point, and a

24

"hawk watch" has been maintained, whenever possible, from mid-September to mid-October. With different weather conditions, an alternate route is used occasionally through Lambton County, crossing the upper end of Lake Erie over Harsens Island; however, efforts to trace flights inland have largely been fruitless. A few sizable groups observed on the Michigan mainland were in the vicinity of Pte. Mouillee and Gibraltar, Wayne County. Very large flights are usually recorded at Holiday Beach on three or four days in fall (6,000 to 10,000); occasional huge numbers (24,000 on September 18, 1974, and 34,700 on September 16, 1970) are associated with a frontal passage and northwest wind. In 1974 a total of 38,150 was counted, probably the most accurate seasonal total (twenty-seven days coverage). Practically all birds have left the area by mid-October (latest: November 30, 1952); one winter record of a bird in St. Clair County on February 1, 1972.

After a pair had been observed in summer of 1968 in Lambton County, a nest with three eggs was found on June 3, 1971. In mid-June of 1974 three young were banded from a nest in Oakland Township, Oakland County. Birds have also been seen in St. Clair County during nesting season in 1972 and 1974.

Swainson's Hawk
Buteo swainsoni

Accidental. A bird of this western species was identified at Pt. Pelee on April 27, 1968 (Kleiman).

Rough-legged Hawk
Buteo lagopus

Winter visitant. Present in winter in varying numbers; most numerous in Lambton County. Reported from mid-September, but not common until November. Generally reported singly or in very small numbers; one exception was a movement of sixty-seven birds following the lakeshore in Kent County on December 28, 1970. Gradual withdrawal in April; a few May reports (latest: May 30, 1945). Two out-of-season records of single birds on July 29, 1951, and August 20, 1950.

Golden Eagle
Aquila chrysaetos

Rare transient, somewhat more numerous after 1960. One bird reported in March, two in August, and two in December. All others (a total of forty-one birds) in fall migration, usually at Pt. Pelee and Holiday Beach (five birds in Michigan counties).

Bald Eagle
Haliaeetus leucocephalus

Rare permanent resident. Steadily decreasing numbers (from a high of fourteen birds in summer of 1951). Possibly three pair left in nesting season: Essex County (Arner and Pelee Island) and Kent

25

County (Rondeau); these have nested in recent years with varying success. Earliest occupied nest was reported on February 9, 1952, at Pt. Pelee. No influx noted in fall; an average of three birds reported in fall in recent years.

Marsh Hawk   *Circus cyaneus*

Uncommon migrant; rare resident. Spring migration evident from early March through May, but in decreased numbers in recent years. Fall migrants present from early September through mid-October; present in largest numbers on regular hawk route, particularly at Pt. Pelee and Holiday Beach (103 in fall of 1973, 194 in fall of 1974). Reported in small numbers in winter. An albino of this species was seen at Rondeau on August 31, 1969.

Formerly bred in fair numbers, probably in all survey counties; however, very scarce recently with most being reported in summer in extensive marsh area of Harsens Island. A nesting pair was present at Metrobeach in summer of 1974; a pair was also present in St. Clair County without nesting evidence. Nests are placed on the ground, often in wet situations; from four to six eggs are laid, usually in last half of May. Earliest: May 12, 1954, a nest with four eggs; latest: July 24, 1955, three young recently out of the nest.

Family PADIONIDAE. Ospreys

Osprey   *Pandion haliaetus*

Uncommon migrant, most numerous in fall. Except for one early arrival date (March 18, 1952), migrants generally arrive in early April and are present into June (latest: June 20, 1970, Rondeau). One summer record of a bird on July 14, 1965, near Milford, Oakland County. Fall migrants scarce before September (earliest: August 18, 1962) then present until late November (latest: November 26, 1950). Generally good numbers in fall, particularly at Holiday Beach (sixty-two in fall of 1974), Pt. Pelee, and Rondeau, but seen also at inland lakes.

Family FALCONIDAE. Falcons

Gyrfalcon   *Falco rusticolus*

Accidental. Two birds reported from Kettle Point; the first was a dark-phase bird on October 29, 1967 (Rupert and John) and the other, a gray-phase bird, on October 27, 1971 (Ryff).

Peregrine Falcon   *Falco peregrinus*

Rare migrant. One or two birds recorded each spring (earliest: March 25, 1950), most in May (latest: June 3, 1969). Somewhat more

26

numerous in fall (usually six to twenty birds, total, each fall), but especially so in 1965 when twenty-four birds were reported from Pt. Pelee.

Merlin *Falco columbarius*

Rare migrant. Very few spring records (total of twelve birds), all from April 23 to May 19. One summer record on August 7, 1954, from Dover Township, Kent County. Reported in fall in small numbers (total of one to ten birds) except for an unusual number in 1964 when twenty-two birds were seen at Pt. Pelee and Holiday Beach. Fall records from September 8 to October 20 (1965), most in last half of September.

American Kestrel *Falco sparverius*

Common migrant; fairly common permanent resident. Regularly reported in all seasons, with migration evident after mid-September during the annual hawk movement. Good numbers move along shore of Lake Erie toward the Detroit River; in the fall of 1974 about 1,040 were counted at Holiday Beach.

Breeds in moderate numbers throughout area, sometimes in urban communities. Eggs are laid in last half of April or early May; young usually on the wing by early July. Nests placed in natural cavities or nesting boxes at various heights (earliest: March 15, 1973, pair at nest site, Oakland County). One pair nested in a Purple Martin (*Progne subis*) house with two nests of Starlings (*Sturnus vulgaris*). Four or five eggs constitute a full clutch. Latest record: August 15, 1954, adults with two fledged young.

Family TETRAONIDAE. Grouse

Ruffed Grouse *Bonasa umbellus*

Permanent resident. Reported throughout year in moderate numbers varying with cyclic population changes. Most Michigan reports from northern Oakland, Macomb, and St. Clair counties. Generally scarce in Canadian counties.

Breeds locally in varying numbers, reduced in recent years; lack of suitable habitat evidently limited nesting to northern-most counties. Eggs may be laid in late April, more often during first half of May (latest: July 8).

Family PHASIANIDAE. Quails, Pheasants, Old World Partridges

Bobwhite *Colinus virginianus*

Common permanent resident. Reported regularly throughout year, but with considerable fluctuation in winter population numbers. Recent increase noted in Lambton County (eighty-six birds on 1974 Breeding Bird Survey in Sombra Township).

Breeds in varying numbers, sometimes locally common. Breeding records from May to September, inclusive (earliest: May 19, 1952, adults with six newly-hatched young, Petersburg, Monroe County; latest: September 14, 1950, nest with thirteen eggs, Wallaceburg, Kent County—abnormally late). Large clutches are usual; two nests reported with nineteen and seventeen eggs.

Ring-necked Pheasant   *Phasianus colchicus*

Introduced. Common to abundant permanent resident; numbers vary from year to year. Sometimes found in large groups in winter, often roosting in trees after snowstorms; maximum of 250 on January 11, 1954.

Breeds commonly. Recorded in all survey counties but less numerous in Ontario except on Pelee Island where it reaches maximum abundance. Nesting begins in late April (earliest: April 24, 1951, nest with ten eggs, Otter Lake, Oakland County). Interrupted nesting or second broods may extend season into early September (latest: September 10).

Gray Partridge   *Perdix perdix*

Introduced. Three birds seen east of Wheatley on May 11, 1950 (Reynolds). No recent sightings.

Family MELEAGRIDIDAE. Turkeys

Turkey   *Meleagris gallopavo*

Once a permanent resident, but extirpated from survey area before 1900. Reintroduced in 1950 when six birds were released at Smith Lake, Lambton County. Subsequently, twenty-five birds were seen in Warwick Township. Not reported since; probably no longer present.

Family GRUIDAE. Cranes

Sandhill Crane   *Grus canadensis*

Rare migrant and summer resident. Records indicate an increase since 1963, including successful nesting of a pair near Holly, Oakland County, in 1969; this corresponds with an increase in numbers nesting in usual sites in counties adjacent to the survey area during the last several years. Recorded twice in Canadian survey counties: a bird at

Pt. Pelee on May 12, 1967, and a bird at Wallaceburg, Kent County, from March 31 to April 15, 1973. Most reports occur during spring migration.

Family RALLIDAE. Rails, Gallinules, and Coots

King Rail   *Rallus elegans*

Uncommon migrant and summer resident. Records indicate a general decrease in recent years despite considerable field work in suitable habitats. Earliest spring arrival: April 20, 1949. Only fourteen fall records. Reported twice in the winter (latest: February 25, 1953, a bird caught in a muskrat trap in Dover Township, Kent County).

Breeds sparingly. Ten actual nest records, four since 1962 (earliest: May 4, 1947, nest with incomplete clutch of three eggs, Oak Park, Oakland County; latest: August 1, 1965, adult with three downy young at Pt. Pelee).

Virginia Rail   *Rallus limicola*

Regular migrant and summer resident. Spring migration most evident during first three weeks of May (earliest: April 17, 1954). Numbers decrease in September, scarce thereafter. Scattered winter records, all in December and January, increasing since 1968; maximum of five birds in winter of 1973–74. A bird was found in open water in the same culvert in northern Oakland County on six consecutive Christmas counts.

Breeds throughout area, sometimes in small marshes; less numerous in Canadian counties. Full clutches of seven to eleven eggs may be found by third week of May (earliest: May 13, 1947, nest with eggs, Oak Park, Oakland County), with the peak of season in first half of June (latest: August 7, 1966, adult with five downy young at Pontiac Lake).

Sora   *Porzana carolina*

Locally common migrant and summer resident, less so since 1960. Few migrants before late April (earliest: April 10, 1966, and April 11, 1945). Fairly numerous through May. Except for two December records (latest: December 28, 1970, Kent County), none reported after late October.

Breeding status, habits, and distribution similar to those of Virginia Rail (*R. limicola*), but slightly more numerous. Nesting begins in late May (earliest: May 23, 1953, nest with eggs, Cranbrook campus), and is usually over by mid-July. However, a nest with four eggs was found in Kent County on August 2, 1968, hatching two days later.

29

Yellow Rail *Coturnicops noveboracensis*

Three records for this secretive and rare migrant. One was seen at Pte. Mouillee on May 9, 1948 (McDonald); one was banded at Pt. Pelee on May 12, 1956 (Gunn); and the third was picked up dead (specimen UMMZ) in Oakland Township, Oakland County, on April 18, 1964 (Carter).

Purple Gallinule *Porphyrula martinica*

A bird was picked up dead (specimen saved) along Eighteen Mile Road in Sterling Township, Macomb County, on June 22, 1973 (Notebaert).

Common Gallinule *Gallinula chloropus*

Common summer resident; abundant fall migrant. Spring migrants generally arrive in mid-April (earliest: April 3, 1965) and remain numerous through May. Reported in large numbers (1,000 to 2,000) during the fall in September and early October in suitable habitats. Three November records (latest: November 23, 1967).

Breeds commonly in deep and shallow marshes on hummocks or floating mats; recorded in all survey counties. Nesting usually begins in mid-May (earliest: May 9, 1973, nest with eggs at Pt. Pelee; May 24, 1974, adult with two downy young at Metrobeach). Eight to twelve eggs are usual, but a nest at Bradley's Marsh had eighteen eggs. The season extends into late summer; four records in late August and September (latest: September 19, 1964, adult with several small young at Big Creek, Essex County).

American Coot *Fulica americana*

Abundant migrant; common summer resident. Winter birds augmented by migrants in mid-March; numerous through May. With the influx of migrants in early September, the species becomes abundant through mid-November, with flocks from 2,000 to 5,000. Numerous winter reports.

Breeds commonly but locally in all survey counties, generally preferring larger marshes than Common Gallinule (*Gallinula chloropus*). Most reports show seven to ten eggs, with nesting common after late May (earliest: May 15, 1953, nest with eight eggs, St. Luke's Marsh, Kent County; latest: September 10, 1966, adult with two downy young in Big Creek marshes, Essex County).

Family CHARADRIDAE. Plovers and Turnstones

Semipalmated Plover *Charadrius semipalmatus*

Fairly common migrant. Spring migrants scarce before mid-May (earliest: April 29, 1962), common through the month; few stragglers into June (latest: June 18, 1950). Largest groups (up to 100 birds) reported from Bradley's Marsh and other extensive marshes. Fall migration begins in mid-July (earliest: July 10, 1949), heaviest from late August to late September, decreasing abruptly after early October. Scattered late records to November 1, 1971.

Piping Plover *Charadrius melodus*

Uncommon migrant; rare summer resident previous to 1953. Regularly recorded in May (one unusually early date: April 4, 1953) at Pt. Pelee, Erie Marsh, Rondeau, and Ipperwash Beach in very small numbers. Very few fall records (latest: September 22, 1963, and September 22, 1967, both at Pt. Pelee).

No breeding records since 1953; the extensive undisturbed beaches used for nesting have largely disappeared. Known to breed regularly at Rondeau prior to 1947, and at Metrobeach for three years prior to 1953. Nesting dates are recorded from May 7, 1952 (nest with four eggs, Metrobeach) to July 10, 1953 (pair with two downy young at Ipperwash Beach).

Killdeer *Charadrius vociferus*

Common migrant and summer resident. Migration begins in late February, heavy by mid-March. Common through fall into early November, occasionally in numbers from 100 to 200. Scattered winter records, most in December.

Breeds commonly. Nests with normal sets of four eggs recorded from April 8 (nest with eggs) to August 9, 1954 (young still attended by adult, Pontiac Lake). Three instances of successful unusual nestings on graveled roofs and one on a hummock in an aspen (*Populus* sp.) woods.

American Golden Plover *Pluvialis dominica*

Regular migrant. Migration noted from mid-April through most of May in varying numbers (earliest: April 6, 1948). Flocks up to 200 birds reported from fields near Pt. Pelee, Bradley's Marsh, and Erieau (Kent County). One unusual record of 2,000 in a corn stubble field in Dover Township, Kent County, on April 24, 1954. Latest: May 28, 1950. Although migrants usually appear in mid-August (earliest: August 5, 1954), they are common only from mid-September through mid-October. Five November records (latest: November 29, 1952).

Black-bellied Plover *Pluvialis squatarola*

Regular migrant. Spring migration begins in late April (earliest: April 21, 1974 and continues through May with a few June records.

31

One record on July 6, 1974. Several groups of 200 to 500 birds were reported, but in the spring of 1973 a flock of about 1,500 birds was seen in Essex County on May 13 and one of 1,300 birds in Kent County on May 17. Fall migration begins in late July (earliest: July 30, 1964), increases through September and October, and diminishes in November (latest: November 28, 1953).

Ruddy Turnstone *Arenaria interpres*

Regular migrant, most numerous in spring. Spring migration from mid-May (earliest: May 9, 1953) through mid-June (latest: June 20, 1970). Maximum of 500 at Erie Marsh on May 21, 1965, and 400 at Pt. Pelee on September 25, 1962. Five July records (earliest: July 6, 1974) with migration most evident from early August through November (latest: November 28, 1953).

Family SCOLOPACIDAE. Woodcock, Snipe, and Sandpipers

American Woodcock *Philohela minor*

Fairly common migrant and summer resident. Arrives about mid-March (earliest: March 5, 1966, 1973, and 1974); uniformly reported thereafter, usually singly or in very small numbers. Regularly reported in fall (latest: November 28, 1964).

Breeds regularly in varying numbers in all survey counties. Almost invariably four eggs are laid (earliest: April 21, 1968, nest with eggs, Lambton County), seldom later than the second week in May (latest: July 10, 1954, adult with four young, Troy Township, Oakland County).

Common Snipe *Capella gallinago*

Fairly common migrant. Spring migration usually begins in late March (earliest: March 14, 1971), heaviest from mid-April to mid-May; two June records (latest: June 6, 1971). Fall migrants generally reappear after mid-July (earliest: July 8, 1973), increasing until mid-August; uniformly recorded through mid-November. Three December records and one in February.

Whimbrel *Numenius phaeopus*

Regular migrant, rare in fall. Except for two June records (latest: June 6, 1971), all were reported from May 17 through 31. Majority of spring reports from vicinity of Rondeau; maximum of 600 on May 23, 1970. Very few fall reports, mostly one or two birds (latest: November 4, 1971).

Upland Sandpiper *Bartramia longicauda*

Uncommon migrant and summer resident. Although numbers fluctuated from year to year (high of sixty-eight in 1946), the over-all population has been greatly reduced in recent years. Spring migrants generally reported near mid-April (earliest: April 14, 1946). Few fall records (latest: October 5, 1963).

Breeds irregularly and locally; new nest records in Lambton and Wayne counties since 1968. Earliest: May 29, 1973, nest with four eggs; latest: July 17, 1954, two young banded, Pontiac Lake.

Spotted Sandpiper *Actitis macularia*

Common migrant and summer resident. Birds arrive about mid-April (earliest: April 11, 1948) and remain numerous through May. Numbers decrease abruptly around mid-September, with scattered reports until late October (latest: October 26, 1952). Generally recorded in small numbers, but occasionally in flocks of 40 to 100, notably at Pt. Pelee.

Breeds commonly; widely distributed. Nests found in gravel pits, on sand beaches, and in other similar situations, often in Common Tern (*Sterna hirunda*) colonies. The usual set of four eggs is occasionally laid by the last week of May (earliest: May 21, 1953, incomplete set of two eggs) but more often after the first week of June. A few reports of unhatched eggs as late as mid-July. Latest breeding record: August 1, 1953, three flying young attended by adults, Ipperwash Beach.

Solitary Sandpiper *Tringa solitaria*

Fairly common migrant. Spring birds appear during last half of April (earliest: April 14, 1954) and are conspicuous until late May (latest: June 3, 1953). More numerous in southward migration (scattered reports of as many as ten to twenty) which begins about mid-July (earliest: July 10, 1971). Migration continues through August and most of September. Two October records and one on November 13, 1953.

Greater Yellowlegs *Tringa melanoleucus*

Common migrant. Somewhat less numerous than the Lesser Yellowlegs (*T. flavipes*). Generally arrives in late March or early April (earliest: March 19, 1966) and is present through May. One record on June 30, 1951. Birds reappear in mid-July (earliest: July 6, 1968) and are recorded through November. Two December records: December 1, 1964, Belle Isle, and December 31, 1966, Pt. Pelee.

Lesser Yellowlegs *Tringa flavipes*

Common migrant. Average arrival around mid-April with two March dates (earliest: March 18, 1945); present through late May and recorded once on June 13, 1972. Fall migrants appear in July (earliest: July 3, 1968) and are numerous in August, diminishing from September through early November (latest: November 16, 1953).

Willet   *Catoptrophorus semipalmatus*

Migrant, previously rare but more numerous since 1962. Reported only four times from 1948 to 1962, seven times from 1962 to 1967, then each year through 1974, including seven birds at Pt. Pelee from May 5 to 17, 1968. An unprecedented twenty-three birds were seen at Stein's Marsh, north of Pt. Pelee, on April 28, 1974. Five fall records; all others in late April and May.

Red Knot   *Calidris canutus*

Uncommon migrant. Reported in the spring from May 17 to June 7; maximum of twenty birds. One July record (July 27, 1974); remainder from August 18 to October 27; maximum of twenty-five at Erie Marsh on September 8, 1973.

Purple Sandpiper   *Calidris maritima*

Rare migrant. Ten reports of single birds from 1945 through 1974, from November 6 through December 23; most from Pt. Pelee, Rondeau, and Kettle Point. One report of four birds at Rondeau on December 4, 1974.

Pectoral Sandpiper   *Calidris melanotos*

Common migrant. Migration evident in spring from late March (earliest: March 20, 1968) in greatly varying numbers. Large flocks include: 400 birds at Bradley's Marsh on April 21, 1968, and 375 at North Cape, Monroe County, on April 3, 1971. Latest spring birds reported on May 30, 1945 and 1952. Fall migration begins in early July (earliest: July 4, 1974), is heaviest in August through early September, then decreases through the latest date, November 22, 1947. Maximum numbers in the fall were flocks of 85 and 110 birds.

White-rumped Sandpiper   *Calidris fuscicollis*

Uncommon migrant, rare before 1963. From one to nine birds reported in spring from May 12 to June 15. Fewer reports of fall migrants. Recorded from September 1, 1956, to a late report on November 12, 1967, at Kingsville, Essex County.

34

Baird's Sandpiper   *Calidris bairdii*

Uncommon transient, rare in spring. Spring migrants recorded from May 14 (1966) to June 7 (1969); maximum of ten, most from Pt. Pelee and Erie Marsh. Regularly reported in the fall from July 30, 1967, to the latest date, November 16, 1968. Maximum for fall was forty-three birds in 1974.

Least Sandpiper   *Calidris minutilla*

Common migrant. Present in spring during May (earliest: May 4, 1950) with one late record on June 5, 1973. Numerous during fall migration from earliest date (July 4, 1974) through mid-November (latest: November 17, 1949, except for a bird at Belle Isle on December 5, 1970). Maximum of 400 at Erie Marsh on July 22, 1973.

Curlew Sandpiper   *Calidris ferruginea*

Accidental. A bird was present at Pte. Mouillee from May 5 to 8, 1975 (found by Falk; seen by Kleiman, Greenhouse, and others). (The rarity of this occurrence warrants inclusion even though later than stated date of period of this publication.)

Dunlin   *Calidris alpina*

Common migrant. Most recorded from May 10 to 30; one early record on April 23, 1949, and two June records (latest: June 20, 1970). Maximum in spring of 700 birds in 1971. Returning migrants reported from July 6, sometimes in large numbers; maximum of 1,500 at Bradley's Marsh. Several reports in November and six in December (latest: December 28, 1971).

Semipalmated Sandpiper   *Calidris pussilus*

Common migrant. Present in spring from early May (earliest: May 2, 1954) through latest date, June 15, 1963. Southward migration begins about mid-July (earliest: July 9, 1949), heaviest through August and September, and decreases in October through latest date, October 24, 1965. Occasionally numerous in fall, especially at Erie Marsh (maximum of 400 on July 23, 1967).

Western Sandpiper   *Calidris mauri*

Uncommon migrant, rare in spring. Single birds in three spring periods in Essex and Lambton counties. Latest: June 4 to 10, 1969, a bird near Sarnia. Reported in small numbers in fall (earliest: August 18, 1970), most from marshes of Monroe County, Pt. Pelee, Rondeau, and Sarnia.

Sanderling *Calidris alba*

Common migrant, most numerous in fall. Reported in spring from May 9 through early June. Fall migrants appear regularly after mid-July (earliest: July 2, 1952) and are numerous in August and September. Numbers decrease in October and November, with three December records.

Dowitcher (sp.) *Limnodromus*

Fairly common migrant, most numerous in fall. Because of the difficulty in species identification in the field of the Long-billed Dowitcher (*L. grisseus*) and the Short-billed Dowitcher (*L. scolopaceus*), they are not separated in survey reports. Although generally reported in small numbers in the spring (May 11 to 21), there was one record of a large number (78 birds) at the Erie Shooting Club, Monroe County, on May 16, 1964, and one of 65 birds at Pt. Pelee on May 15, 1974. Returning migrants reported from July 6 through October 24. Several reports of 80 to 220 birds in fall.

Stilt Sandpiper *Micropalama himantopus*

Regular migrant, rare in spring. Reported more frequently, particularly in the fall, after 1962. Few spring records (earliest: May 12, 1967). Reported on fall migration from July 8 (1973) through October 31. Several groups of twenty-five to forty birds since 1968.

Buff-breasted Sandpiper *Tryngites subruficollis*

Uncommon migrant. Reported more frequently and in larger numbers since 1970. A total of 106 birds reported in the fall of 1973; maximum of 35 at Pt. Pelee on September 1. Only one spring record (May 31, 1952); remainder from late August through September.

Marbled Godwit *Limosa fedoa*

Rare migrant. Only three records before 1965; thirteen records of fifteen birds from 1965 through 1974. Reported three times in May, once in April, and remainder from August 10 to latest date, October 13.

Hudsonian Godwit *Limosa haemastica*

Rare migrant. Somewhat more numerous than preceding species (*L. fedoa*). Three spring reports, two in the vicinity of Pt. Pelee on May 12, 1956, and May 25, 1974, and one in Erieau, Kent County, on June 20, 1970. Recorded in fall from August 19 (1972) to November 21 (1971) in very small numbers (one to four birds) except for a group of eleven birds at Erie Marsh on September 26, 1970.

36

Ruff *Philomachus pugnax*

Rare vagrant, but of more frequent occurrence in recent years. First recorded on April 28, 1965, a male found in Ft. Gratiot Township, St. Clair County (Lamb); collected on April 29 (UMMZ), first state record. Reported since as follows: May 12, 1967, Wheatley; September 27, 1969, River Canard, Essex County; May 1971, two different males at Bradley's Marsh; September 11 to 18, 1971, Pte. Mouillee; May 6, 1972, Erie Marsh; May 13, 1973, Pt. Pelee; August 17, 1974, Erie Marsh.

American Avocet *Recurvirostra americana*

Rare visitant. First seen and photographed at Erie Marsh from May 18 to 20, 1963 (Kleiman and Horton). Nine subsequent occurrences, reported in spring only in May and in fall from August 9 to October 26. An unprecedented number of twenty-four birds was seen at Pt. Pelee on May 4, 1968; a second large group of ten birds was present at St. Luke's Marsh, Kent County, from September 24 to 27, 1974.

Red Phalarope *Phalaropus fulicarius*

Rare migrant. Seven records of this normally pelagic migrant. Single birds were reported from Canadian counties as follows: November 2 and 3, 1965, Ipperwash Beach (Rupert); November 16, 1969, Pt. Pelee (Kleiman and Wilson); October 15, 1970, Pt. Pelee (Maley); October 18,1970, Wheatley (Rupert and others); October 23 to 26, 1973, Rondeau (Chesterfield and Pratt); November 16 and 23, 1974, Kettle Point (Rider); and December 13, 1974, Pt. Pelee (Morin).

Wilson's Phalarope *Steganopus tricolor*

Uncommon migrant; rare summer resident. Very scarce before 1964, regular thereafter in small numbers of one to five. All spring reports were in May and are less numerous than fall when it is recorded through late September (latest: September 26, 1966); reported from large marshes in Essex, Kent, Monroe, and Wayne counties.

Nested two seasons at Kettle Point (earliest: July 23, 1967, nest with one newly-hatched young). Two nests in 1968, one unsuccessful.

Northern Phalarope *Lobipes lobatus*

Uncommon migrant, rare in spring. Three spring reports: two in late May and one on June 7, 1969, all at Erie Marsh. Regularly reported in fall (earliest: August 25, 1973); most in September and October.

Family STERCORARIDAE. Jaegers

Pomarine Jaeger *Stercorarius pomarinus*

Specific identification of four birds, all in fall of 1973, as follows:

one at Pt. Pelee on October 13 (Rupert); one on St. Luke's Bay, Kent County, on October 30 (Schlageter); and two at Kettle Point on November 9 (Rider).

During the fall of 1973 an unusual influx of thirty-one jaegers was reported, most at Kettle Point and Pt. Pelee, of which twenty-three were reported as *Jaeger* (sp.) due to difficulty of field identification of Pomarine and Parasitic Jaegers. Besides the twenty-three noted above, twenty-two others have been reported to the survey as *Jaeger* (sp.). All were recorded along the shores of the Great Lakes and have been more numerous since 1970.

Parasitic Jaeger   *Stercorarius parasiticus*

First recorded at Pt. Pelee on September 29, 1966 (Wasserfall); bird later found dead. Fourteen records of twenty-four thereafter, most at Pt. Pelee or Kettle Point in October; reported also at Rondeau and in Monroe County (one bird at Sterling State Park on July 4, 1972).

Long-tailed Jaeger   *Stercorarius longicaudus*

One found dead (skeleton UMMZ), badly decomposed, at North Cape, Monroe County, on September 21, 1963 (Ligon and Jehl).

Family LARIDAE. Gulls and Terns

Glaucous Gull   *Larus hyperboreus*

Uncommon but regular winter visitant, more numerous since 1960. Most recorded from November into May (one early date: September 29, 1974, at Pt. Pelee) along St. Clair River and Lake Huron, with some records from Pt. Pelee and Lake Erie marshes. Frequently found at garbage dumps and sewage outfalls along waterways. Latest: May 13, 1960.

Iceland Gull   *Larus glaucoides*

Rare but regular visitant. Distribution similar to preceding species, but reported less often. Reported from late November through spring, but most after late February (latest: June 8, 1969, Kettle Point). Most adults are probably referable to the race *kumlieni*.

Great Black-backed Gull   *Larus marinus*

Regular visitant. Gradual increase in numbers after the early 1940s, evidently because of expansion of range. Regularly recorded from late September into May, most in December, with several concentrations of 100 to 200 birds, particularly in Lake Erie marshes. Scattered records in July and August, but no evidence of breeding.

Thayer's Gull   *Larus thayeri*

Authorized as separate species from Herring Gull (*L. argentatus*) by the *Thirty-second Supplement to the American Ornithologists' Union Check-list of North American Birds*. It is suspected that a few of the gulls reported may refer to this species, but until authoritative guides to identification are available, none is listed as this species.

Herring Gull   *Larus argentatus*

Abundant permanent resident. Found along Great Lakes and connecting waterways in all seasons, but least numerous in June and July despite sizable but local non-breeding flocks. Becomes abundant in August (up to 3,000) and remains so through fall. Numbers vary in winter, depending largely on the amount of open water.

Breeding records are from Lake Erie islands, Essex County: fifteen occupied nests on Middle Sister Island on July 5, 1952 and forty occupied nests on Chicken Islands in 1954. Single nests with eggs in southeastern Monroe County in 1953 and 1956. Recent records refer to two successful nests at Kettle Point in 1968 and three newly-hatched young at the same location on July 7, 1974.

Ring-billed Gull   *Larus delawarensis*

Abundant permanent resident. Heavy influx in fall but reduced numbers in winter. Sizable non-breeding population in summer. May be found inland, particularly in winter.

At least one pair was found breeding with Common Terns (*Sterna hirundo*) on Bob-Lo Island in the Detroit River in 1961; one downy young banded on July 22, 1961 (Nickell). There were eleven occupied nests at Ipperwash Beach on July 5, 1964. A small colony of twelve nests with eggs was present on Mud Island in the lower Detroit River on June 24, 1967; by early July of 1972 the colony had increased to 500 adults.

Black-headed Gull   *Larus ridibundus*

Accidental. Two reports of this old-world species, both from tip of Pt. Pelee: one on May 6, 1960 (Hamel and Holland) and the second on May 18, 1973 (Rupert).

Laughing Gull   *Larus atricilla*

Rare vagrant. Reported only in spring and summer. First recorded at Erie Marsh on May 21, 1965 (Kleiman). Five later records, four of them in 1973 and 1974, from Pt. Pelee, Wheatley, Port Franks (Lambton County), and Erie Marsh (Greenhouse, John, Kleiman, and Rupert).

Franklin's Gull   *Larus pipixcan*

Migrant, rare in spring, uncommon in fall. Reports have increased since the late 1960s. Recorded most frequently from western Lake Erie but occasionally from southern Lake Huron. Scattered spring reports, generally of adult birds, most from Pt. Pelee.

A bird in breeding plumage was present at Rondeau through the summer of 1970.

Bonaparte's Gull   *Larus philadelphia*

Abundant spring and fall migrant. Large numbers in April and May (up to 15,000 in 1973). Scattered summer reports. Numbers build up in September, reaching a peak in late fall and winter (up to 7,000 in late December 1971); reported into January in suitable winters.

Little Gull   *Larus minutus*

Uncommon visitant; occasional summer resident. First survey report of a bird at Pt. Pelee from May 10 to 12, 1962; however, there are unreported records of the species at Rondeau in 1957. Regularly and increasingly reported in spring since 1962; smaller numbers in fall into early January.

In 1970 three pairs nested at Rondeau (July 12). Small numbers summer there most years (thirty-five in 1974).

Ivory Gull   *Pagophila eburnea*

Accidental. An immature bird was seen near Grosse Ile, Trenton Channel, on January 12, 1949 by Van Camp and others (Zimmerman and Van Tyne, 1959).

Black-legged Kittiwake   *Rissa tridactyla*

Rare visitant. One bird at Port Huron on December 19, 1945 (Kiefer). Not reported again until November 7, 1967, when one was collected at North Cape, Monroe County (Tordoff; specimen UMMZ). At least eight records since (one to three birds) from early November through mid-December (latest: December 17, 1971). Reported from Pt. Pelee, Lake Huron, and Lake Erie.

Sabine's Gull   *Xema sabini*

Accidental. Reported only in 1974 as follows: a bird seen at Erie Marsh on November 29 (Maley and others); one at Pt. Pelee on October 14 and 29 (Morin).

Forster's Tern   *Sterna forsteri*

Regular migrant, locally common. Reported in small numbers in spring, largely from Pt. Pelee. Fall migrants reported by late July in good numbers (100 to 300 birds) through fall into November. Summers regularly at Walpole Island (Kent County) and St. Clair Flats and occasionally at Rondeau. Young fledged birds have been recorded annually along the St. Clair River just north of Walpole Island, indicating the species probably nests somewhere in the St. Clair Flats.

Common Tern

Sterna hirundo

Abundant migrant; common summer resident. Appears in spring about April 1 (earliest: March 24, 1952 and 1962), abundant by third week. Somewhat less numerous in fall, but a few reports of large numbers (10,000 in Monroe County on September 19, 1971). A huge movement of this species with gulls was seen on August 27, 1972, when Rupert and Rider estimated 24,000 terns moved past Marentette Beach, Essex County, with about as many present in the nearby fields.

Breeds locally in generally good numbers, evidently reduced on some islands because of recent high water levels. Colonies vary in size from a few pairs to several hundred; vegetational changes or human interference may cause them to change or leave a location. Records show eggs are sometimes laid by mid-May (earliest: May 7, 1952, three nests with incomplete sets of eggs, Metrobeach) but the peak of the season is from the second week in June through the month (latest: August 9, 1959). Nests occasionally are placed on muskrat houses or floating mats of marsh vegetation instead of the usual hollows in dry situations. Most recent record refers to thirteen nests with young or eggs at Kettle Point on July 6, 1974.

Caspian Tern

Hydroprogne caspia

Common migrant. Present in spring from mid-April (earliest: April 14, 1954); numerous around mid-May. Scattered reports through June and early July after which they increase in numbers until September. A few October reports (latest: October 23, 1965).

Black Tern

Chlidonias niger

Uncommon summer resident, formerly common. Most numerous along the Great Lakes but also found inland. Scattered arrival dates before early May (earliest: April 7, 1952), numerous thereafter. Present throughout summer, with largest groups in July and August; no recent reports of 200 or more as reported prior to 1960. Numbers diminish from late August through September; three October dates (latest: October 18, 1950).

Breeds in suitable marshes throughout area; however, no recent records from the Lake Erie marshes. Breeding still known to occur in the St. Clair Flats, Rondeau, and the Pt. Pelee area. Nests frequently on muskrat houses, floating mats, or windrows of marsh vegetation.

41

Two to four eggs are laid, usually in early June (earliest: June 1, 1973, nest with three eggs, Pt. Pelee; latest: July 23, 1949, nest with two eggs, Pte. Mouillee). Recent records show decline in breeding populations because of high water; there were only eight nests at Pt. Pelee in 1973 compared to twenty-seven in 1972, a result of the flooding of mud flats.

Family ALCIDAE. Murres

Thick-billed Murre   *Uria lomvia*

Accidental. A bird of this species was captured alive on a street in Royal Oak, Oakland County, on November 29, 1950, by Walmer and brought by Tenhave to Nickell at the Cranbrook Institute of Science, where it later died (UMMZ). A second of these sea birds, found dead at New Baltimore, Macomb County, on November 23 of the same year, was later identified by Nickell (UMMZ). Both birds, doubtless, were driven inland by a severe November storm.

Family COLUMBIDAE. Pigeons and Doves

Mourning Dove   *Zenaida macroura*

Common permanent resident. Reported most often in April and May, but occasionally found in large flocks (100 to 200 birds) in winter.

Breeds abundantly, in rural and urban areas; well distributed. Nests reported each month from February to October, inclusive. Earliest: February 13, 1969, nest with two eggs (later abandoned); latest: October 4, 1973, two nests; both in Wayne County. Frail nests, almost invariably with two eggs, are placed in a variety of situations; four reports of nests on the ground.

Family CUCULIDAE. Cuckoos and Anis

Yellow-billed Cuckoo   *Coccyzus americanus*

Fairly common summer resident. Migrants arrive in early May (earliest: May 2, 1954), common by mid-month. Most have left by the end of September. Eight October records; two in November (latest: November 8, 1963).

Breeds regularly in moderate numbers, although somewhat reduced in recent years. Most of the active nests are recorded from mid-June to third week in July (earliest: May 30, 1952, a nest with three eggs, Pontiac Lake). A few scattered reports in August (latest: August 26, 1953, nest with two young and one unhatched egg, Roseville, Macomb County). This species and the Black-billed Cuckoo (*C.*

42

erythropthalmus) may lay one or more eggs, not always distinguishable, in the nests of the other. There was one noteworthy record of a Yellow-billed Cuckoo apparently successfully parasitizing a nest of the Red-winged Blackbird (*Agelaius phoeniceus*).

Black-billed Cuckoo   *Coccyzus erythropthalmus*

Summer resident, less common than the Yellow-billed Cuckoo (*C. americanus*). Arrival generally noted about mid-May (earliest: May 6, 1950). In the fall numbers diminish gradually in September; six October records (latest: October 25, 1969, a bird picked up dead on the shore of Lake Huron following a storm).

Breeding status, distribution, and habits similar to previous species. One nest with seven eggs (photographed), perhaps laid by two females. Earliest record: May 27, 1952, nest with one egg and one young; latest: August 13, nest with three eggs; both Bloomfield Hills, Oakland County.

Family TYTONIDAE. Barn Owls

Barn Owl   *Tyto alba*

Uncommon permanent resident, scarce in the 1960s, but reported more regularly since 1970, mainly from Monroe County, Bradley's Marsh, and Pt. Pelee.

Has bred irregularly in small numbers, but practically absent in recent years; recent records only from Bradley's Marsh in 1968 and from rural Monroe County in 1973 and 1974. Artificial nesting boxes placed in the latter area produced an increase to four nesting pairs in 1974.

Family STRIGIDAE. Typical Owls

Screech Owl   *Otus asio*

Fairly common permanent resident. Regularly reported in all seasons from all survey counties. Little migratory movement evident except for an influx of thirty-six birds reported in the winter of 1969-70.

Breeds regularly, but distribution and nesting dates poorly defined. Reported nesting in six of eight counties. Earliest: April 17, 1964, nest with eggs in barn, Gosfield Township, Essex County; latest: June 28, 1954, dead young of the year. One nest in Oakland County in a Wood Duck (*Aix sponsa*) nest box hatched five young on May 9, 1970, with the birds still in box (banded) on May 22.

Great Horned Owl   *Bubo virginianus*

Fairly common permanent resident. No seasonal fluctuation or movement noted. Reported largely in extensive wooded areas.

Breeds regularly; reported in all counties but Monroe; somewhat more numerous in Lambton County (seven nests in 1970). Nesting regularly begins earlier than for any other species with possible exception of the Horned Lark (*Eremophila alpestris*). Normally two eggs are laid in the last half of February or early March, often in abandoned or usurped nests built by crows, hawks, or herons. Earliest nest: February 5, 1967, Lambton County; two late records: July 7, 1954, a young owl able to fly but with down in plumage, Milford, Oakland County; June 29, 1963, three young out of nest unable to fly, Columbus Township, St. Clair County.

Snowy Owl   *Nyctea scandiaca*

Winter visitant, erratic and uncommon, but recorded each year. Largest flights occurred in winters of 1949–50 (thirty-three birds) and 1971–72 (thirty-six birds). Single birds occasionally linger into spring (recorded in April and May at Ipperwash Beach) and once into summer (a bird at Metrobeach through spring and summer of 1951, evidently sick or wounded, found dead in mid-August).

Barred Owl   *Strix varia*

Rare permanent resident. Reported in all seasons most often from Oakland County; only four winter records.

Three breeding records, two from Oakland County and the most recent from Port Huron Game Area on June 2, 1969. May also breed at Rondeau.

Long-eared Owl   *Asio otus*

Uncommon resident. Reported most often in fall and winter, singly or in family groups. Occasionally found in larger numbers in suitable habitats such as pine plantations (maximum of twenty-five).

Breeding status and distribution not well defined; recent records only from Stony Creek Metropark. Earliest: April 11, 1954, adult flushed from nest, Port Huron Game Area; latest: June 10, 1970, five young in nest at Stony Creek Metropark.

Short-eared Owl   *Asio flammeus*

Regular winter visitant. Reported in fall and winter after late October, occasionally in groups of ten to twenty-five which may remain for some time in vicinity of airports, plantations, and similar locations. One or two reports of birds until late April or early May. One summer record of a bird at Rondeau on June 25, 1950, but no breeding records.

Saw-whet Owl *Aegolius acadicus*

Regular migrant. Status and distribution not well known, probably due to secretive habits. Banding operations since 1962 have shown regular fall migration at inland locations in Oakland County and at Pt. Pelee. Special projects at the latter location have resulted in the banding of 300 birds in one season during October and November. One unconfirmed report of a nest with four young near Wallaceburg, Kent County, in 1965.

Family CAPRIMULGIDAE. Goatsuckers

Whip-poor-will *Caprimulgus vociferus*

Uncommon migrant; rare summer resident. Spring arrival near mid-April (earliest: April 16, 1949); migration continues through May. Very few fall records (latest: two October records and one at Pt. Pelee on November 3, 1962).

Two breeding records, both from Lambton County: June 16, 1964, nest with two young at Ipperwash Beach; June 25, 1974, nest with two young hatching at Kettle Point. Several summer records indicate nesting in St. Clair County; summer records also from Rondeau, Grosse Ile, and three stations in Oakland County.

Common Nighthawk *Chordeiles minor*

Abundant migrant; common summer resident. Spring migration usually begins in early May (earliest: April 30, 1950). Fall migrants observed in evening flights soon after mid-August, heaviest through early September, often in very large numbers. In 1974 about 5,420 birds were counted on September 7 at three stations, with a total of more than 9,000 birds for the fall season. Several October dates; latest: October 22, 1966.

Breeds commonly, widely distributed, but with very few actual nest records; majority referred to eggs or young on gravel roofs. Earliest: June 6, 1952, two nests, each with two eggs, Detroit and Chatham, Kent County; latest: September 23, 1966, a young bird barely able to fly, Oakland County.

Lesser Nighthawk *Chordeiles acutipennis*

Accidental. A bird was seen and photographed at Pt. Pelee on April 29, 1974 (Wormington).

Family APODIDAE. Swifts

Chimney Swift *Chaetura pelagica*

Common migrant and summer resident. Birds scarce in spring

before late April (earliest: April 16, 1972), numerous thereafter. Numbers decrease rapidly during last ten days of September, but reported in large groups earlier in the month (up to 1,000). Four October observations, one later (November 7, 1959).

Breeds commonly, but few nests examined; most records refer to occupied sites or sounds of young birds in chimneys. Earliest nest: June 6, 1954, occupied nest in St. Clair County; latest: August 3, 1953, two young banded.

Family TROCHILIDAE. Hummingbirds

Ruby-throated Hummingbird *Archilochus colubris*

Common summer resident. Numerous after mid-May (earliest: April 25, 1962). Large numbers at Pt. Pelee (maximum of 200 on May 11, 1963). Fall migration heavy in September (maximum of 350 on September 14, 1952, also at Pt. Pelee), decreasing in October (latest: October 17, 1968, and October 18, 1954).

Breeds regularly, widely distributed, but few actual nests found. Nesting seldom begins before first week in June (earliest: June 2, 1965), with renestings or second broods extending season well into July or early August (latest: August 20, 1966, nest with two young, Kent County; another nest, August 20, 1970, St. Clair County). Nests are placed at moderate heights in a variety of trees, often in dooryards or orchards, but also in remote woodlands.

Rufous Hummingbird *Selasphorus rufus*

Accidental. A bird of this western species was present in Chesterfield's yard near Wheatley from August 7 to 9, 1972.

Family ALCEDINIDAE. Kingfishers

Belted Kingfisher *Megaceryle alcyon*

Common summer resident. Spring migrants common after late March; reported uniformly throughout summer and early fall at inland waters and larger marshes. Numbers decrease after mid-October, but reported in winter in varying numbers.

Breeds regularly, widely distributed. Earliest record: April 17, 1952, female excavating a nest burrow, Macomb County; latest: July 8, 1954, adult with three recently fledged young, Bosanquet Township, Lambton County.

Family PICIDAE. Woodpeckers

Common Flicker (Yellow-shafted Flicker)   *Colaptes auratus*

Common summer resident; winters regularly in varying numbers. Spring migration evident after mid-March; birds abundant in April and May, with large numbers reported at Pt. Pelee (100 to 125), Bradley's Marsh, and Rondeau. Numerous again in September, decreasing after mid-October; regularly reported in winter (108 in winter of 1971–72).

Most abundant breeding woodpecker, widely distributed. Nesting may be in boxes, natural cavities, or excavations in dead trees. Nest sites may be started or refurbished in late April, but normal sets of six to eight eggs are seldom completed before the second week in May. Latest: August 6, 1949, adult feeding one fledged young, Monroe County.

Pileated Woodpecker   *Dryocopus pileatus*

Casual visitant; rare summer resident. One or two birds reported each year, most consistently from Rondeau, where they evidently breed. Reported also from Columbus Township (St. Clair County), Proud Lake Recreation Area, and Ipperwash Beach. A pair raised young near Camlachie, Lambton County, in 1969, the only actual breeding record.

Red-bellied Woodpecker   *Centurus carolinus*

Regular visitant, most common in winter; rare summer resident. Very few birds reported before 1960, but a consistent increase thereafter, especially in winter (thirty-five in winter of 1971–72). First recorded nesting at Pt. Pelee in 1967; also in Holly Township, Oakland County, on May 21, 1967, and each year thereafter. Undoubtedly nests at Kensington Metropark where it has been reported in all seasons, as well as at other local stations.

Red-headed Woodpecker   *Melanerpes erythrocephalus*

Summer resident, locally fairly common. Migration evident from mid-April through May with the largest numbers at Pt. Pelee. Reported in considerable numbers also in fall, particularly at Pt. Pelee and Holiday Beach. Most have left by late October, but scattered reports are regular in winter.

Breeds in varying numbers, but less numerous in recent years; especially common at Rondeau. Few nests examined. Four to six eggs are laid, usually in late May or early June. Earliest record: May 5, 1952, adults excavating nest cavity, Holly Township, Oakland County; latest: August 23, 1964, four young being fed in nest, Oakland Township, Oakland County.

Lewis' Woodpecker *Asyndesmus lewis*

Accidental. One was present from February 6 through March 10, 1973, at Ojibway Park, Windsor, Essex County; identified and photographed (Wilson) and seen by many observers.

Yellow-bellied Sapsucker *Sphyrapicus varius*

Fairly common migrant; rare summer resident. Spring migration usually begins in early April, heaviest until mid-May. Fall migration evident from mid-September to late October. Scattered records in November and through winter (fourteen in winter of 1971–72).

Three breeding records, all from Port Huron Game Area, none recently. Nest records as follows: June 5, 1954, adults at active nest; June 4, 1955, an occupied nest; June 23, 1956, pair feeding young at nest site. Summer records from Pt. Pelee on June 23 and August 2, both in 1952.

Hairy Woodpecker *Dendrocopos villosus*

Fairly common permanent resident. Recorded uniformly throughout year, but varying somewhat from year to year, particularly in fall and winter.

Breeds regularly, but in moderate numbers; no records from Monroe or Essex counties. No nests examined; all reports refer to occupied nests located primarily in swamp forest habitats or to adults with fledged young. Earliest: May 11, 1952, adults bringing food to young in nest, Thamesville, Kent County; latest: July 25, 1954, adults with fully-grown young, Port Huron Game Area.

Downy Woodpecker *Dendrocopos pubescens*

Common permanent resident, more numerous than Hairy Woodpecker (*D. villosus*). Reported generally throughout area, but less frequently in summer during breeding season when birds withdraw to more rural areas. Winter birds conspicuous at feeders.

Breeds throughout area. Nest sites may be excavated or under repair in late April, but full clutches of four or five eggs are seldom completed earlier than mid-May. Latest record: July 25, 1954, adults with three fully-grown young, Lynn Township, St. Clair County.

Black-backed Three-toed Woodpecker *Picoides arcticus*

Rare visitant. A mild invasion reported in fall and winter of 1953–54 when nine birds were recorded in Lambton and Macomb counties and at Grosse Ile. Since then single birds were seen at Pt. Pelee (October 27, 1956, and April 7, 1973), at Mt. Clemens (from December 5 to

19, 1968), and in Lambton County (October 27, 1974); three birds were present at Rondeau in December 1974.

Northern Three-toed Woodpecker   *Picoides tridactylus*

Accidental. One was found on December 24, 1974, at Pt. Pelee where it remained throughout the winter (Chesterfield).

Family TYRANNIDAE. Tyrant Flycatchers

Eastern Kingbird   *Tyrannus tyrannus*

Common summer resident. Migrants appear in late April (earliest: April 22, 1964); numerous after May 1. Large numbers reported at Pt. Pelee (twenty to seventy birds) both in spring and fall migrations. Most migrants leave the area in September; two October reports (latest: October 7, 1954).

Breeds commonly in survey area, mainly in upland habitats but sometimes in wet situations. Nests occasionally built in mid-May (earliest: May 18, 1968) but majority recorded from second week in June to mid-July; most late summer records probably represent renestings. Latest date: August 20, 1950, adults attending two fledglings, Bradley's Marsh.

Western Kingbird   *Tyrannus verticalis*

Accidental. Five records of single birds. Four birds seen in Essex County as follows: Pt. Pelee, May 19, 1956, and September 11, 1958; Big Creek, September 15, 1957; and Holiday Beach, September 13, 1964. One Michigan-area record of a bird at Erie Marsh on August 14, 1966.

Scissor-tailed Flycatcher   *Muscivora forficata*

Accidental. A bird was seen at Pt. Pelee on June 3, 1961 (Mara), the only survey record for this species.

Great Crested Flycatcher   *Myiarchus crinitus*

Common summer resident. Spring migrants numerous by early May (earliest: April 14, 1968). Fall migration begins in early September, largely over by end of month. Two October records: October 9, 1951 and 1953.

Breeds regularly throughout area, but not verified in all counties. Nesting begins in late May (earliest: May 26, 1952), reaches peak in mid-June, and is usually over by third week in July (latest: August 1, 1953, adults with fledged young). Nest sites range from unused

49

mailboxes and nest boxes at low elevations to natural tree cavities at considerable heights.

Eastern Phoebe   *Sayornis phoebe*

Summer resident. Before 1957 the species was common in migration, with several reports of twenty to seventy birds at Pt. Pelee; since then, following a disastrous spring migration and probably other undetermined factors, it has not regained any semblance of its former numbers. Spring migrants usually appear about mid-March (earliest: March 4, 1959). Fall migration is late, with little decrease until late October. Four November records and three in December (latest: December 24, 1972).

Breeding population greatly decreased, now limited to local stations, notably Stony Creek Metropark and the more northerly sections of the survey area. Earlier records show that nesting usually begins in late April (earliest: April 12, 1953) or early May, with later broods or renestings, often in the same nest (seventeen records), extending the season well into August. Records show that five eggs were laid in 75% of the first nests of the year. Cowbird parasitism in the 324 records previous to 1960 was more than 10%.

Yellow-bellied Flycatcher   *Empidonax flaviventris*

Uncommon transient. Increased banding activities in recent years have added considerable data on migration periods and abundance for this species and others of the *Empidonax* group. Less numerous in spring than fall (earliest: April 29, 1964); latest spring migrants were banded on June 4, 1964 and 1966. Banding records also indicate earlier fall arrival than previously known; three July records (earliest: July 10, 1968) and four August records. Fall migration usually is over by end of September, with three October banding records (latest: October 25, 1973).

Acadian Flycatcher   *Empidonax virescens*

Uncommon and local summer resident. Arrival mainly after mid-May (earliest: May 9, 1954). Few fall records (latest: September 4, 1946 and 1954). One record on August 29, 1954, from St. Clair County which is north of normal range.

Breeds locally in small numbers in Oakland, Macomb, and Kent (most common at Rondeau) counties. May be overlooked at other favorable locations because of indistinctive song and quiet breeding behavior. Semipensile nests, usually built after mid-June, are placed at moderate heights in deciduous trees, most frequently in well-shaded, undisturbed woodlands. Earliest record: May 26, 1951, adult at a newly-completed nest, Pontiac Lake; latest: August 18, 1957, adult feeding well-grown cowbird, Davisburg, Oakland County. Three of the thirty-five records, or 8.6%, showed cowbird parasitism.

Traill's Flycatcher   *Empidonax trailii*

Common summer resident. Migrants appear in early May (earliest: May 3, 1969), common by May 20. Regularly reported throughout summer, but most fall records were identified only as to genus. Two separate species are now authorized by the *Thirty-second Supplement to the American Ornithologists' Union Check-list of North American Birds*. These are based on "fee-bee-o" song type (*E. alnorum*) and the "fitz-bew" song type (*E. trailii*). Until more than one season has elapsed to allow for the checking of song types in the survey area, the former collective designation is used.

Records indicate that this is the most abundant breeding flycatcher; less numerous in Ontario counties. Usually four eggs are laid in first nests of year which seldom are completed before the first week in June (earliest: May 25, 1953, nest under construction). Because of renestings and possible second broods, eggs may be found as late as the third week in July and young in the nest well into August (latest: August 29, 1953). Of 253 nest records, 16, or 6.34%, were parasitized with one or two cowbird eggs covered in nest linings or in abandoned nests. One report of a small cowbird in a nest, but no record of successful fledging.

Least Flycatcher   *Empidonax minimus*

Local summer resident, most common in Lambton County. Spring migration evident through May (earliest: May 1, 1948 and 1950). Fall migration heaviest in September, with a few early October records (latest: October 8, 1948).

Breeding status and distribution poorly defined. The few definite nest records refer to occupied but unexamined nests or to adults feeding young (earliest: June 26, 1954, adults feeding half-grown young).

Eastern Wood Pewee   *Contopus virens*

Common summer resident. Spring migrants common by mid-May (earliest: April 26, 1974). Fall migration mostly over by end of September; a few October records (latest: October 30, 1960).

Breeds commonly. First nests of year may be started in late May, with peak in mid-June. Nearly all nests were recorded in horizontal positions several feet from main trunk of large trees. Earliest: May 24, 1954, nest under construction; latest: September 1, 1951, adults feeding fledged young, Utica, Macomb County.

51

Western Wood Pewee *Contopus sordidulus*

Accidental. A singing bird was identified at Pt. Pelee on May 17, 1968 (Baillie and Chesterfield).

Olive-sided Flycatcher *Nuttallornis borealis*

Uncommon migrant. Reported in spring from May 10 to June 13, most in late May. Five July and August records. Fall migration most evident in September, but continues into October (latest: October 18, 1966).

Family ALAUDIDAE. Larks

Horned Lark *Eremophila alpestris*

Abundant migrant; common resident. Migration heavy in February and March. Fall migrants numerous from mid-September through November. Present throughout winter in varying numbers (maximum of about 1,000 along roadsides in Kent County on January 14, 1968).

Breeds commonly throughout area. Nesting begins very early, often while snow is still on the ground (earliest: February 16, 1968, nest with three eggs). Nearly half the reports refer to nests excavated in sod on golf courses, loose sandy areas, and similar exposed situations of barren patches and relatively short grass. Latest: August 15, 1950, adult feeding fledged young. One report of parasitism by cowbirds.

Family HIRUNDINIDAE. Swallows

Tree Swallow *Iridoprocne bicolor*

Common summer resident. Migrants usually arrive in late March (earliest: March 18, 1972), abundant from mid-April through May. Found in large flocks in summer after nesting season (2,100 at Harsens Island in July). Numbers decrease gradually through September; some scattered large groups in October (900 on October 19, 1968). Latest: December 8, 1974.

Breeds commonly, particularly near water. Occasionally nests in semicolonial situations (twenty-six pairs occupied unused mail boxes on Harsens Island on June 11, 1946). Nests may be in natural tree cavities, unused woodpecker holes, or in nest boxes, often using boxes erected to attract Eastern Bluebirds (*Sialia sialis*). One record of a pair occupying a nest in the same willow stub with a pair of Starlings (*Sturnus vulgaris*). Several records of two broods in one season (earliest: April 13, 1970, an active nest at Stony Creek Metropark; latest: July 7, 1973, adults feeding five young at Northville, Wayne County).

Bank Swallow   *Riparia riparia*

Abundant summer resident. Except for one very early date (April 7, 1951), arrival generally reported during last ten days of April. Large concentrations (1,500 to 10,000 birds) from mid-July through August at Pt. Pelee, Metrobeach, and Ipperwash Beach. Numbers diminish rapidly in late September (latest: October 2, 1949).

Most abundant breeding swallow in area. Colonies widely distributed, varying in size from a few pairs to several hundred. In 1954 large numbers were banded at several nesting colonies, and the contents of sample nests were recorded, using a light and mirror arrangement (Nickell and Stapp). The data showed that in thirty-three June nests, clutch size averaged 5.2 eggs; in seventy-eight July nests, the average was 4.36 eggs. Earliest record: May 13, 1950; latest: July 18, 1954; both Cranbrook campus.

Rough-winged Swallow   *Stelgidopteryx ruficollis*

Fairly common summer resident. Spring migrants scarce before mid-April (earliest: April 4, 1954), common by early May. Concentrations reported in last half of August and early September, particularly at Pt. Pelee (100 to 500 birds). Most leave by mid-September. Scattered records in October include 50 birds on October 5, 1974 (latest: October 12, 1958).

Breeds regularly in fair numbers. Occasionally nests in association with Bank Swallows (*Riparia riparia*) in tunnels excavated by the latter, but more often nests in drain tiles and similar man-made situations. Two records of nests with large masses of leaves and twigs in open garages. Nests may be started in late May (earliest: May 18, 1953, an occupied nest, Oakland County), but normal clutches of five or six eggs are not usually laid before the second week in June. Interruptions and renestings may extend season (latest: August 2, 1953, nest with three young).

Barn Swallow   *Hirundo rustica*

Common summer resident. Arrival usually noted in mid-April (earliest: April 5, 1954), with migration heavy through May. Birds gather in flocks (up to 150) during August; most leave area in September. Several October records, two in November (November 6, 1971, and November 25, 1973).

Breeds commonly throughout area. Nesting usually begins in late May (earliest: May 14, 1947, occupied nest, Oakland County) and continues throughout the summer with occasional two broods (latest: August 22, 1954, nest with young). Three instances of colonial nesting: seven nests under same bridge near Utica, Macomb County, in 1951 and 1952; five nests under a bridge in Lambton County in 1968.

Cliff Swallow *Petrochelidon pyrrhonota*

Uncommon migrant and summer resident. Earliest arrival date: April 5 and 6, 1970. Reported in small numbers in spring (season total varies from 6 to 16 birds with high seasonal total of 33 birds in 1952). Somewhat larger numbers in fall. One unusual record of 250 birds in Kent County on August 18, 1969. Latest: October 4, 1964.

Breeds irregularly and locally, reported in all survey counties. Most records refer to active, unexamined nests or adults with fledged young. Earliest: May 15, 1953, St. Clair County; latest: July 22, 1950, adults feeding one young, Monroe County.

Purple Martin *Progne subis*

Common summer resident. Average arrival recorded in early April (earliest: March 21, 1966), numerous by late April. Large flocks reported in August and early September (1,500 to 6,000), somewhat reduced in recent years. Most leave by late September, but recorded twice in mid-October (latest: October 20, 1949).

Breeds commonly, widely distributed, but tending to greater abundance near bodies of water. Because of inaccessibility, most records refer to active colonies or adults with fledged young. Apparently only one brood is raised, usually in June, but interruptions may delay final attempts until well into July. Cold weather in 1973 caused many young to die in the nest. Birds reported at nest sites as early as May 8, 1974, at Pontiac, Oakland County, and May 19, 1967, at Pt. Pelee. Latest: August 12, 1951, Ipperwash Beach and August 11, 1972, Oakland County, adults with fledged young.

Family CORVIDAE. Jays, Magpies, and Crows

Gray Jay *Perisoreus canadensis*

A bird was collected at Pt. Pelee in July 1969 (Wyett), the first survey record. Two birds were again present at Pt. Pelee on October 11, 1972; one was captured and banded.

Blue Jay *Cyanocitta cristata*

Common resident; abundant migrant. Migration evident during late April and first half of May; largest numbers recorded along Great Lakes at Pt. Pelee, Ipperwash Beach, and other locations in groups of 100 to 500. Fall migration has been given considerable attention since 1950, together with the hawk migration. Large numbers are often present at Pt. Pelee, crossing Lake Erie; however, the highest counts were made in the vicinity of Holiday Beach where they cross the Detroit River near its mouth, often directly over Grosse Ile. Large groups are also seen at Bradley's Marsh and Harsens Island; presence at the latter station indicates a more northerly crossing into Michigan. This large-scale migration generally extends from mid-September through early October. Total fall counts varied greatly, probably reflecting somewhat the amount of field coverage; in five fall periods since 1960, totals varied from 83,000 to 156,000 birds. High daily counts varied from 7,000 to 23,000. Jays are common in the survey area during winter. Banding records indicate that at least part of the local winter population is different from the summer population; winter birds may be replaced by returning migrants, some of which constitute the summer population.

Breeds regularly throughout the area. Nesting sometimes begins in April (earliest: April 4, 1954, nest being built, Avon Township, Oakland County) but more often in early May, with height of season from late May until third week of June. Four or five eggs are laid. No definite evidence of more than one brood per season. Latest: August 13, 1973, adults feeding young in nest area, Detroit. Observed post-nesting behavior included a new nest completed in a leafless maple (*Acer* sp.) in November, 1949, at Dearborn, Wayne County, and a bird carrying nesting material into a white pine (*Pinus strobus*) on November 18, 1953 (Miller).

Black-billed Magpie   *Pica pica*

Accidental. A bird was present at Pt. Pelee from January 12 into February 1973 (seen by many observers).

Common Raven   *Corvus corax*

Rare visitant. From one to four birds were present at Ipperwash Beach in the fall of 1969 (first seen on October 19). Single birds reported at Pt. Pelee from October 4 to 11, 1970, and at Kettle Point on October 20, 1974.

Common Crow   *Corvus brachyrhynchos*

Abundant migrant; common resident. Winters in large numbers, particularly in Essex County (75,000 estimated in late fall of 1974); smaller numbers (3,000 to 11,000) in Macomb and Wayne counties. Migration evident in late February through March, mainly in Canadian counties (20,000 along Lake Huron on March 29, 1972). Regular through summer.

Breeds commonly throughout area. Nests usually completed and normal clutches of four or five eggs laid by mid-April (earliest: April 2, 1953, nest under construction), but majority of reports were for first half of May. Latest record: July 22, 1950, adult with two well-grown young.

Family PARIDAE. Chickadees and Titmice

Black-capped Chickadee   *Parus atricapillus*

Common permanent resident and migrant. Numbers vary greatly because of irregular invasions. A heavy influx was reported in October of 1951 (up to 300) at Pt. Pelee with some remaining through the winter, although many crossed Lake Erie. A second such invasion occurred in the fall of 1954 when five times the normal number were reported (a total of 1,580 birds). In October 1972 a similar movement took place, this time accompanied by unusual numbers of Boreal Chickadees (*P. hudsonicus*). A smaller migration was reported in the early winter of 1965. Migration is also evident in spring in smaller and variable numbers.

Breeds in moderate numbers. Nests with normal sets of six to eight eggs reported from May 2 to July 5. Five July dates suggest occasional second broods. One report of an adult feeding a fully-fledged cowbird. An unusual nest site in a pipe of a teeter-totter on a playground in Oakland County was reported in 1972.

Boreal Chickadee   *Parus hudsonicus*

Rare and irregular fall and winter visitant. Four reports of single birds outside of years of large invasions of Black-capped Chickadees (*P. atricapillus*), these in 1947, 1969, and 1970. During the 1951 invasion, about thirty birds were reported, primarily from Canadian counties. The largest influx was reported with the invasion of 1972–73 when birds were present throughout the survey area; at Pt. Pelee sixty-nine were banded from October 11 to November 10, and in the Michigan counties forty-five birds were reported from eight stations. A few birds appeared to remain into spring during each invasion (latest: May 10, 1973).

Tufted Titmouse   *Parus bicolor*

Common permanent resident in Michigan counties, rare in Canadian counties. Only three reports in Canadian counties before 1955; since 1966 one to three birds have been reported each year, most in winter, suggesting an extension of range.

Breeds regularly; nest records from Lambton County in 1965 and Essex County in 1967. Most reports refer to nest-building activities or adults with fledged young. The one nest examined was in a nest box and had seven eggs on May 24, 1953. Earliest record: April 21, 1953, a pair building a nest; latest: July 16, 1969.

Family SITTIDAE. Nuthatches

White-breasted Nuthatch   *Sitta carolinensis*

Common permanent resident. Largest numbers reported in winter, probably due to presence at feeders (maximum of eighteen birds).

Breeds locally in moderate numbers. Because of inaccessible location of nests, most reports refer to occupied sites or adults with young. Two nests in boxes contained eight eggs on May 8 and five young on May 30. Earliest record: April 19, an occupied nest; latest: July 19, adults with two young.

Red-breasted Nuthatch   *Sitta canadensis*

Irregular transient and winter visitor. Fall migrants usually appear in late August, most common in September and October; small numbers remain through the winter. Numbers vary greatly from year to year; heavy influx in fall of 1969, but practically absent in 1974.

One actual breeding record, probably the southernmost in state. A nest discovered thirty feet up in a willow (*Salix* sp.) stub on the Cranbrook campus on May 18, 1952 (Nickell); later, adults observed carrying food to young in the nest. Near this site a bird was observed working on a nest cavity from April 18 to 25, 1954 (Nickell); he banded one young barely able to fly, also in the same general location, on July 7, 1965. A pair was present at Westcroft Gardens on Grosse Ile through the summer of 1965, suggesting breeding. Other summer records include a bird at Rondeau on July 6, 1963, and three July and early August records in Oakland County.

Family CERTHIIDAE. Creepers

Brown Creeper   *Certhia familiaris*

Common winter resident; rare breeder and summer straggler. About mid-September birds become numerous as they do again in April (up to forty birds at Pt. Pelee and Bradley's Marsh); most have left by the end of May. However, since 1965 one or more birds have been reported each year in late June and early July at Pt. Pelee, Rondeau, Metrobeach, and five stations in Oakland County. In the summer of 1974 birds were seen in four locations in Oakland County, most in typical breeding habitats.

One actual nest was located at Pt. Pelee on July 19, 1962 (Chesterfield). Two adults were seen feeding young at a nest under a loose strip of bark about eighteen feet up in a high stump in a wet woods. Adults were seen throughout summer by several observers. Before this publication went to press, a nest with five young was found at Highland Recreation Area on June 6, 1975 (Greenhouse).

Family TROGLODYTIDAE. Wrens

House Wren   *Troglodytes aedon*

Common summer resident, somewhat reduced in recent years. Arrival dates vary considerably from year to year, usually before April 25 (earliest: April 13, 1954). Sometimes present in good numbers at migration points, such as Pt. Pelee and Rondeau (twenty to thirty-five birds). Common until end of September after which numbers diminish rapidly. Four November dates and one late straggler on December 24, 1972, at Pt. Pelee.

Breeds commonly throughout area, most often in and about rural and urban communities but frequently in remote wooded areas. Nests are placed in all manner of nooks and crannies, often in odd situations. One found at Beach-o-Pines, Lambton County, was in a discarded gallon can that was buried in the ground except for the exposed spout; the six young left the nest upon discovery but were caught and banded. Nesting normally begins about the third week in May; second broods are regularly raised in late July or the first half of August. Earliest nesting date: April 25, 1974, pair building nest; latest: September 3, 1973, young leaving nest, Oakland County.

Winter Wren   *Troglodytes troglodytes*

Fairly common migrant, occasionally numerous; uncommon winter resident. Fall migrants generally arrive in mid-September (earliest: August 29, 1954); several reports of good numbers at Pt. Pelee and Bradley's Marsh in the fall (maximum of 200 on September 30, 1972). Reported throughout winter, most often before January, and in spring through May. One summer report of a singing male at Highland Recreation Area on July 8, 1973.

Bewick's Wren   *Thryomanes bewickii*

Rare migrant and summer resident. Reported in spring from April 3 to May 25 (total of twenty-two records since 1945). All records are from Pt. Pelee except the following: single birds on May 1, 1963, St. Clair Shores, Macomb County; on May 2, 1969, Wayne County; and on April 19, 1972, East Sister Island, Essex County. Besides breeding records, there is one summer report (August 12, 1952) and two in fall (September 17 and October 7, 1950).

Four breeding records at Pt. Pelee (Gunn), as follows: a nest with eggs in mid-May 1956, broken up soon thereafter; three singing males and three nests in various stages of construction from May 9 to 15, 1957. Apparently none of the nests was successful, but one in 1957 had four eggs before being abandoned some time prior to May 15. No breeding evidence since.

Carolina Wren   *Thryothorus ludovicianus*

Permanent resident, uncommon to rare. For some years prior to 1970 the species had become very scarce, but there are some indications of an increase since then. Reported throughout the area, most frequently from Pt. Pelee. Most numerous in winter, with largest recent numbers (eighteen birds at Pt. Pelee and ten elsewhere) in the winter of 1973.

Four breeding records before 1955, one in 1965, and two (same pair) in 1974. Scarce breeding dates show a nest with five eggs at Rondeau on May 6, 1955, and a nest with two young in a garage in Dearborn, Wayne County, in mid-August 1951. A pair was present in a yard near Rockwood, Wayne County, in summer of 1973; the following summer a pair at this location raised two broods, the first in a nest in an empty coffee can in a shed with access only through a small opening in a broken window.

Long-billed Marsh Wren   *Telmatodytes palustris*

Common summer resident. Arrival usually after mid-April. Three early dates: March 28, 1971; April 1, 1964; and April 4, 1967. Locally common throughout summer; especially numerous at extensive marshes around Harsens Island, Bradley's Marsh, and the marshes of upper Lake Erie. Numbers diminish in late September, but scattered later records include nine December reports (maximum of five at Pt. Pelee on December 24, 1972) and two in February.

Breeds commonly throughout area. Unlined or "dummy" nests may be built in late May, but few occupied nests reported before second week in June. Numerous reports of examined nests indicate that normally five or six eggs are laid. Scattered July dates (latest: July 20, 1952, nest with three eggs, Pt. Pelee) indicate that usually only one brood is raised.

Short-billed Marsh Wren   *Cistothorus platensis*

Uncommon summer resident, local and more scarce in recent years. Except for reports of migrants at Pt. Pelee (earliest: April 23, 1946), most spring records were from local breeding areas. Regularly reported in suitable habitats throughout summer and fall (latest: October 16, 1971).

Breeds in varying numbers; very scarce from 1960 through 1971, with some indication of increase since then, especially in 1974 when birds were present at four locations. Summer occurrence more often reported from wet meadows or semi-dry situations than typical marsh habitats. Earlier records included a nest with eight eggs in a high heavy pasture, Mersea Township, Essex County, on June 21, 1958. More recent records were a nest with eggs at Pt. Pelee on June 9, 1969, and a semicolonial situation where four nests with four pairs of adults were found at Kettle Point on June 2, 1974. Reported in summer in recent years at Stony Creek Metropark, Port Huron Game Area, and local areas in Monroe and Oakland counties.

Family MIMIDAE. Mockingbirds and Thrashers

Mockingbird   *Mimus polyglottos*

Uncommon visitant and summer resident. Rare before 1962 (only seventeen birds reported), but increasing numbers indicate an extension of range. Since 1962 reported from all counties in all seasons, somewhat more in winter. Maximum number reported: twelve birds in spring of 1974.

Two nesting records prior to 1962. Since then, however, breeding records have been fairly regular, particularly from Sombra Township, Lambton County, where there were four nests in fairly close proximity in 1968. Reported nesting also in Kent, Wayne, Oakland, and Macomb counties. Usually, three to five eggs were reported, with young hatching in mid-June (latest: July 29, 1973, three well-grown young in a nest in Lambton County).

Gray Catbird   *Dumetella carolinensis*

Common summer resident. Spring migrants numerous by late April, with scattered March and early April records. Often present in large numbers of 75 to 100 birds at Pt. Pelee and other migration points. Common throughout summer and fall to mid-October. Scattered records thereafter through mid-January.

Breeds commonly, widely distributed. Nesting begins by mid-May (earliest: May 14, 1949, nest with three eggs), with second broods and renestings extending season into first part of August (latest: August 6, 1949, nest with three young). In a study of 358 nests, Nickell found that 59.5% of first nests have clutches of four eggs, 32.1% have three eggs, and remaining 8.4% have five eggs. Survey records show four instances of cowbird parasitism, only one successful.

Brown Thrasher   *Toxostoma rufum*

Common summer resident. Arrival generally reported in mid-April (one early record: March 18, 1963), with migration heavy through May. Regularly reported until end of October, with scattered records in winter.

Breeds commonly, well distributed. Nests with normal clutches of four or five eggs reported in late May (one record of an early completed nest on April 29, 1969, Bloomfield Township), but most often in first half of June. Nearly half were located in hawthorn (*Crataegus* sp.) or similar thorny situations; three were directly on the ground. Latest date: August 22, 1973, young being fed out of the nest, Oakland County. Three instances of cowbird parasitism reported (one apparently successful), rare for this species.

Sage Thrasher   *Oreoscoptes montanus*

Accidental. One report of this western species at Pt. Pelee on May 12, 1965 (Chesterfield), first Ontario record as well as first survey record.

Family TURDIDAE. Thrushes and Bluebirds

American Robin   *Turdus migratorius*

Common summer resident. Evidently spraying with material containing DDT and other pesticides greatly reduced numbers, but an increase is apparent since spraying was reduced and stopped in many areas. Although good numbers of birds winter in areas of available food, migrants are evident by early March.

Breeds commonly, generally in close proximity to people. Nesting begins in early April if weather is suitable (nests built in first four days of April reported in 1951, 1972 and 1974), but generally in late April or early May. Interruptions or second broods (one record of third brood) may extend season well into August (latest: August 23, 1960). Four eggs are laid in majority of cases, but three and five eggs are not uncommon and there is one report of six eggs. Two instances of cowbird parasitism were reported, neither successful.

Varied Thrush   *Ixoreus naevius*

Accidental. A bird of this western species was present at Rondeau from January 23 to March 24, 1965 (Ussher and others), third Ontario record and first survey record. Three birds have been reported since, seen by many observers; two in the winter of 1968–69, one at Sarnia and one at Proud Lake Recreation Area; the third bird was present in Rouge Park, Detroit, from March 9 to 30, 1971.

Wood Thrush   *Hylocichla mustelina*

Fairly common summer resident. Scattered arrival records in April (earliest: April 10, 1948), but most spring migrants first recorded in early May. Occasionally reported in good numbers (forty to fifty birds) during heavy spring movements of passerines, especially at Pt. Pelee. In the fall birds leave gradually during September and October (latest: November 8, 1969).

Breeds regularly; locally numerous at areas such as Rondeau. Nesting usually begins in late May (earliest: May 14, 1949, nest with three eggs, Lake Orion) and extends through July, with some indications that second broods are raised. Latest date: August 12, 1972, nest with adults present near Rockwood, Wayne County.

Hermit Thrush   *Catharus guttata*

Common migrant. Spring arrival generally noted in early April;

migration largely over by end of May. Earliest fall date: August 10, 1972, a bird banded. Migration heaviest in October, with reduced numbers through early November and scattered records throughout winter.

One breeding record in summer of 1954: a singing male observed in the Port Huron Game Area on June 5 and 6 (O'Reilly); a full-grown young in juvenal plumage, undoubtedly fledged in the immediate vicinity, was found at the same area on June 28 (O'Reilly). Zimmerman and Van Tyne (1959) state that this species is very rare in summer south of the Saginaw and Grand valleys. No summer records since.

Swainson's Thrush   *Catharus ustulata*

Common migrant. Spring migration usually begins in mid-April (one very early report on March 19, 1972), heavy until mid-May, then scattered reports through June 6. Occasionally numerous (50 to 200 birds) at Pt. Pelee, Rondeau, and Bradley's Marsh. Banding activities since 1960 have shown that fall migrants may reach the area earlier than previous sight records indicate: eight July and early August records (earliest: July 16, 1968). Migration heaviest in September, largely over by end of October. Two December records (latest: December 31, 1966).

Gray-cheeked Thrush   *Catharus minima*

Uncommon migrant. Spring migration period corresponds closely to that of the Swainson's Thrush (*C. ustulata*). Earliest: April 19, 1945; latest spring date: May 31, 1953. Fall migrants, however, appear somewhat later (earliest: September 2, 1966). Fall field identification difficult; banding records indicate good numbers in the fall, but fewer than the preceding species (latest: October 20, 1947).

Veery   *Catharus fuscescens*

Fairly common summer resident. Spring migrants arrive in early May (earliest: May 2, 1953); more numerous in spring than fall. Maximum numbers reported (estimated at 500 birds) during a spectacular passerine migration at Pt. Pelee on May 10, 1952. Most birds leave the area in September; a few October records and one of a late bird at Kensington Metropark from November 16 to 18, 1972.

Breeds regularly but locally, most often in extensive, undisturbed woodlands such as Rondeau. Nesting begins in mid-May (earliest: May 14, 1949, nest with two host eggs and two cowbird eggs), with renestings or second broods sometimes extending the season well into July (latest: July 12, 1947, nest with two young). Normal clutches have three or four eggs. Most nests reported from late May to end of June.

Eastern Bluebird   *Sialia sialis*

Uncommon summer resident, formerly much more numerous.

Spring migrants generally recorded in mid-March. Prior to 1957 good-sized concentrations were reported in fall (35 to 200 birds); since then, only one large group (60 birds at Pt. Pelee on November 6, 1971) has been reported. Small numbers usually remain throughout winter, but these numbers have also been reduced in recent years.

Recent data from Pinkowski on 219 nests in Stony Creek Metropark from 1968 through 1974 indicate that nesting may begin in late March (earliest: March 24, 1973, nest under construction; earliest complete clutch: April 8, 1973), but cold weather may cause interruptions. Two broods were raised in 76% of the cases of successful first nests. Second clutches are usually completed from mid- to late June, and renesting may extend egg-laying into July (latest: July 24, 1974, full clutch; latest departure of young from nest: August 24, 1974). Clutches consist of two to six eggs, but four or five eggs are usual; numbers are smaller as season progresses.

Mountain Bluebird   *Sialia currucoides*

Accidental. Two adult females were seen at Pt. Pelee on December 4 and 5, 1965 (Botham; one collected). An adult male was found at Pt. Pelee on December 29,1971 (Wilson).

Townsend's Solitaire   *Myadestes townsendi*

Accidental. One found at Pt. Pelee on March 3, 1962 (Mara and Horton; specimen Royal Ontario Museum).

Family SYLVIIDAE. Gnatcatchers and Kinglets

Blue-gray Gnatcatcher   *Polioptila caerulea*

Fairly common summer resident. Spring arrival generally recorded in last half of April (earliest: April 15, 1974); maximum number of forty reported at Pt. Pelee on May 20, 1971. Less numerous in fall; most in September, four October records (latest: October 27, 1965) and one on November 1, 1960.

Breeds regularly in moderate numbers, but not verified for all counties. Nests usually placed well out on branches of tall trees, making examination almost impossible. Earliest date: May 10, 1964, adults building nest; latest: July 11, 1953, adults feeding two fledglings, Port Huron Game Area.

Golden-crowned Kinglet   *Regulus satrapa*

Common migrant and winter visitant. Arrival usually around mid-September (earliest: September 10, 1952). Most numerous in October as migrants move through, with large numbers reported at Bradley's

Marsh and Pt. Pelee. Reported consistently throughout winter, with increased numbers in spring migration from late March through early May (latest: May 30, 1953).

Ruby-crowned Kinglet   *Regulus calendula*

Common migrant; rare winter visitor. Fall migration usually reported first in late August or early September (earliest: August 24, 1951); heaviest in October, with large numbers of up to 100 birds at various migration points. Although migration is largely over by the end of November, scattered records show that a few (4 to 17 birds) usually remain throughout the winter. Spring migration most evident from mid-April through May (latest: May 30, 1954).

Family MOTACILLIDAE. Pipits

Water Pipit   *Anthus spinoletta*

Fairly common transient. Rare in spring, reported mainly from Ontario counties in very small numbers (earliest: April 4, 1964); latest spring departure date: May 29, 1968. More numerous in fall (earliest: September 27, 1953) with two reports of large numbers (120 in Mersea Township, Essex County, on November 7, 1964, and 200 near Pt. Pelee on November 6, 1966). Four December reports and one on January 5, 1971. In 1973 a bird remained at an Oakland County cemetery from January 30 to March 11.

Sprague's Pipit   *Anthus spragueii*

Accidental. First recorded on May 21, 1960, in Groveland Township, Oakland County (Peters, Postupalsky and others). Another was seen with forty-five Water Pipits (*A. spinoletta*) in Harwich Township, Kent County, on October 2, 1973 (Randall and three others).

Family BOMBYCILLIDAE. Waxwings

Bohemian Waxwing   *Bombycilla garrulus*

Rare winter visitor. Reported in six different years (one to seven birds), three times at Pt. Pelee. Reported most often in January; one report of a single bird at Pt. Pelee on November 10, 1968.

Cedar Waxwing   *Bombycilla cedrorum*

Common migrant and permanent resident. Reported in large flocks of 100 to 500 birds, except during nesting season. An increase in birds in late August and September indicates migration. Wintering populations vary greatly in numbers; virtually absent in some years (only eight birds reported in winter of 1949).

Breeds regularly throughout the area in varying numbers. Nesting normally begins later than any other species with the exception of the American Goldfinch (*Spinus tristis*) (earliest: June 2, 1949, nest with four eggs, Oakland County). Majority of reports show nests built after mid-June, with season continuing throughout summer, occasionally into September (latest: September 7, 1952 and 1953, nests with young, Oakland County). One instance of cowbird parasitism.

Family LANIIDAE. Shrikes

Northern Shrike   *Lanius excubitor*

Irregular winter visitant. Only one substantial invasion reported, beginning in October 1953 and continuing through the winter and spring until mid-April 1954. During this period fifty-four birds were reported (several banded, a few collected) from all counties except Monroe. During other years only small numbers of five to ten birds were observed.

Loggerhead Shrike   *Lanius ludovicianus*

Uncommon summer resident. Records indicate a substantial decrease in numbers in recent years; practically absent in fall. Arrival usually recorded in March (earliest: March 4, 1950); uniformly reported through the rest of spring and summer (latest: September 27, 1953).

Breeds irregularly in varying numbers; no nesting records in recent years. Earlier records indicate nesting may begin in April (earliest: April 18, 1954, an adult at a newly-completed nest, Macomb County), but usually in May. Majority of nests examined had five or six eggs or young and were placed in hawthorns (*Crataegus* sp.) or Osage Orange (*Maclura pomifera*) trees, usually within ten feet of the ground. Latest: July 10, 1954, adults feeding two fledged young, Port Huron Game Area.

Family STURNIDAE. Starlings

Starling   *Sturnus vulgaris*

Introduced species. Abundant in all seasons, but largest flocks reported in fall, numbering from 5,000 to 10,000 birds. One large roost under the north end of the Ambassador Bridge usually numbers in the thousands.

Breeds abundantly throughout the area. Nesting usually begins in late April (earliest: March 22, 1953, a bird building a nest); height of season reached in May with first young often out of the nest by early June. Nests are placed in any cavity that provides protection and concealment, generally at the expense of more desirable species. Records indicate that five eggs constitute a normal clutch. Latest record: August 1, 1952, an occupied nest, Mt. Clemens.

Family VIREONIDAE. Vireos

White-eyed Vireo   *Vireo griseus*

Uncommon migrant; rare summer resident. Formerly rare (six records from 1945 through 1955, all but one from Pt. Pelee in spring); regular in spring since 1959, reported from all counties. Most numerous in spring of 1973 when sixteen birds were reported at Pt. Pelee; several summer reports during the same year. Spring arrivals generally recorded in late April and early May (earliest: April 25, 1970). Very few fall reports (two very late dates: October 28, 1962, a bird banded at Bradley's Marsh, and November 11, 1971, one banded in Oakland County).

During the summer of 1971 two active nests were reported from Rondeau, both unsuccessful.

Bell's Vireo   *Vireo bellii*

Rare and accidental. Two reports before 1963, but reported in seven different years since then; all single birds except for one report of two birds at Rondeau from May 8 to 20, 1971. One record from Grosse Ile, all others from Pt. Pelee, Rondeau, and Bradley's Marsh from May 8 to 22.

Yellow-throated Vireo   *Vireo flavifrons*

Summer resident, locally fairly common. Spring migrants generally reported in late April (earliest: April 19, 1945). Reports indicate that most birds leave the area during the last two weeks in September; a few October records (latest: October 23, 1968).

Breeds locally, distribution not well defined; most nests reported from Oakland and northwest Macomb counties. Because of the inaccessibility of nest locations, none was examined. Earliest: May 14, 1949, adults at a newly completed nest, Lake Orion, Oakland County. Length of season indicates occasional second broods (latest: August 28, 1949, adults feeding three well-grown young, Oakland County). Two reports of cowbird parasitism.

Solitary Vireo   *Vireo solitarius*

Uncommon transient. Most spring reports during first three weeks of May (earliest: April 17, 1971; latest departure: May 27, 1950 and 1951). Less numerous in fall when earliest arrival date was September

1, 1949. Two late departure dates: November 17, 1957, and November 17, 1967 (banded).

Red-eyed Vireo
Vireo olivaceus

Common summer resident. Migrants generally appear during first ten days of May (earliest: May 1, 1954); well distributed by middle of month. Fall reports indicate that species remains common through mid-September, with numbers gradually decreasing thereafter until mid-October. Scattered reports in last half of October, two in November (latest: November 9, 1969).

Breeds commonly, well distributed. Nesting generally begins in early June (earliest: May 26, 1951, adult at a new nest, Oakland County) and reports well into September indicate second broods may be raised (latest: September 12, 1951, adults feeding three well-grown young, Holly, Oakland County). About 63.5% (fifty-two nests) showed parasitism by cowbirds.

Philadelphia Vireo
Vireo philadelphicus

Uncommon transient. Reported in spring from May 9 (1953) to June 2 (1971). Banding operations in recent years indicate the species is more numerous in fall than earlier sight records show. Reported in fall from August 28 (1967) to November 11 (1966).

Warbling Vireo
Vireo gilvus

Common summer resident. Spring arrival generally reported during first week of May (earliest: April 27, 1957 and 1963). In fall most have left by late September. Two reports of stragglers: one bird which remained at Stony Creek Metropark through November in 1967 and a sight record of a bird at Pt. Pelee on November 19, 1974.

Breeds commonly, reported from all counties. Nesting usually begins in late May (earliest: May 12, 1949, a pair at a new nest, Oakland County) and continues into mid-summer (latest: July 19, 1953, adults feeding fledged young, Mt. Clemens). Several reports of incubating males singing on the nest. Dates indicate only one brood is raised.

Family PARULIDAE. Wood Warblers

Black-and-white Warbler
Mniotilta varia

Common migrant; uncommon summer resident. Arrival generally reported during the last ten days of April (earliest: April 15, 1974); migration heaviest the first three weeks of May. Several spring reports of large numbers (35 to 100 birds) and a most unusual concentration (estimated at 1,000 birds) with the unprecedented migration at Pt. Pelee on May 10, 1952. Fall migrants appear in mid-August, regular through September, with scattered reports in October (latest: October 21, 1951).

Breeds locally in small numbers in at least the four northernmost survey counties. Two records of typical, well-concealed ground nests in northern-type habitat: May 28, 1949, nest with young, Lake Orion; June 5, 1954, nest with three warbler eggs and two cowbird eggs, extreme northwest Macomb County. Other reports refer to adults with fledged young or cowbirds on dates from June 24 to July 18. Cowbird parasitism was 37.5%.

Prothonotary Warbler · *Protonotaria citrea*

Rare migrant and summer resident. All except one of the spring reports before 1960 were from Canadian counties. Since then the species has been reported from Monroe, Wayne, Oakland, and St. Clair counties, mostly single records (earliest: May 2, 1970); four banded birds. Very few fall records, all in the last half of August.

Has nested sparingly in Kent, Essex, Oakland, and Macomb counties; nests in the two Michigan counties in 1957 (none since) are believed to be the only modern breeding records for southeastern Michigan. Recent records indicate that Rondeau is the only station where the species nests consistently. Nesting usually begins in late May (earliest: May 16, a pair building at Pt. Pelee) and reaches peak early in June. Cavities in dead stubs in or near water were most frequently chosen sites.

Worm-eating Warbler · *Helmitheros vermivorus*

Rare visitant; reported more frequently since 1965. Seven records before 1965, one from the Cranbrook campus on May 20, 1961, the first Michigan record. Recorded every year except one since 1965; maximum of six birds in 1967 from four counties. Recorded in spring between April 19 (1972) and June 6 (1967), most regularly from Pt. Pelee, but occasional records from all other counties except Monroe and St. Clair.

Golden-winged Warbler* · *Vermivora chrysoptera*

Fairly common summer resident. Average spring arrival between May 5 to 10 (earliest: April 29, 1964). Except for migrants at Pt. Pelee, most were reported from local nesting areas. Reported in gradually reduced numbers during July and August; five September records (latest: September 23, 1950).

---

*Hybrids between Golden-winged and Blue-winged Warblers were reported consistently. The "Brewster's Warbler" was more numerous and was found nesting in Oakland and St. Clair counties. Three reports of the rare "Lawrence's Warbler": May 23, 1948, Wayne County; May 14, 1949, Pt. Pelee; May 20, 1967, St. Clair County (one banded).

Breeds regularly but locally in varying numbers; all records from northern Oakland, Macomb, and St. Clair counties. Generally inhabits moist, undisturbed woodlands or brushy edges near water. Nesting begins in late May or first week in June (earliest: May 18, 1958, female building a nest in a dry situation in northwest Macomb County); mostly over by mid-July. Evidently only one brood is raised (latest: July 18, adults feeding fledgling, Oakland County). Nests are situated on or near the ground (fourteen reports); about twenty reports of adults with fledged young. Cowbird parasitism reported in 26.5% of cases.

Blue-winged Warbler   *Vermivora pinus*

Uncommon summer resident. Arrival generally reported soon after May 1 (earliest: April 27, 1974), mostly from Pt. Pelee and local breeding areas in Oakland and St. Clair counties. Scattered fall reports in late August and a few in September (latest: September 25, 1971).

Breeds in small numbers in Oakland, Macomb, and St. Clair counties (probably also in favorable habitats elsewhere in area). Usually found in association with the more numerous Golden-winged Warbler (*V. chrystoptera*); nesting activity practically identical. Very few nests located (earliest: June 6, 1948, nest with five eggs at Lake Orion; latest: July 10, 1954, adults feeding fledged young, White Lake Township, Oakland County).

Tennessee Warbler   *Vermivora peregrina*

Common transient. Main spring migration between May 10 and 27, with a few late April and early May records (earliest: April 27, 1954; latest: June 4, 1964, bird banded). More numerous in fall migration which generally begins during the last ten days of August (earliest: August 12, 1972). Regular through September and early October (latest: October 31, 1960 and 1966). Two out-of-season records of birds banded on July 20, 1965, and August 1, 1960.

Orange-crowned Warbler   *Vermivora celata*

Uncommon transient. Spring migrants generally reported during second and third week of May (earliest: April 28, 1962; latest: May 25, 1952). Very few fall records until several banders became active about 1954; since then species has been taken regularly in small numbers. Late migrants reported on October 31, 1959; November 6, 1959; and November 4, 1967.

Nashville Warbler   *Vermivora ruficapilla*

Common transient. Spring migrants generally recorded in early May (earliest: April 22, 1968), numerous throughout the month. Sometimes numerous in spring (up to sixty birds), particularly at Pt. Pelee and Bradley's Marsh. Several June records (latest: June 26, 1954, Oakland County). Banding has shown a few individuals may appear very early on southward migration (three records between July 26 and August 6). Bulk of migrants reported in September and early October, with late reports on October 28, 1964, and November 1, 1958. A straggler was seen in Lambton County on December 30, 1967.

Virginia's Warbler   *Vermivora virginiae*

Accidental. A bird of this western species was identified at Pt. Pelee on May 16, 1958 (Dow and Gray) and later collected (Stirrett; specimen National Museum of Canada), the first Canadian record. A second bird was present from May 9 to 11, 1974, at Pelee Island (Broughton and others). Before this publication went to press, another bird was found at Pt. Pelee on May 3, 1975 (Greenhouse; photographed by Rupert and seen by many observers).

Northern Parula   *Parula americana*

Uncommon transient. Arrival usually recorded in early May (earliest: April 22, 1964). Migration through the month (latest: June 6, 1971), with one out-of-season record at Highland Recreation Area on June 30, 1974. Most numerous in spring with several reports of eight to ten birds at Pt. Pelee. Fall migrants reported in mid-September (earliest: September 12, 1945) and generally are present until late October. Two November records: November 6, 1971, Oakland County, and November 23, 1961, Pt. Pelee.

Yellow Warbler   *Dendroica petechia*

Common summer resident. Numerous in spring soon after arrival during last few days of April (earliest: April 18, 1954), with large numbers (100 to 300 birds) reported at Pt. Pelee, Rondeau, and Bradley's Marsh. Numbers decrease sharply soon after mid-August; however, banding has provided a number of late records from September 8 to 20. One very late bird was banded at Bradley's Marsh on October 22, 1966.

Most numerous and widely distributed summering warbler, although somewhat reduced in recent years. A previous population reduction in early 1950s seemed to be temporary. Nesting may begin by mid-May (earliest: May 10, 1953, nest with five eggs) with normal clutches of four or five eggs reported by the end of the month; height of season about second week in June. Normally only one brood is raised, but excessive cowbird interference or other interruptions may delay final attempts until early July (latest: July 23, adults feeding a full-grown cowbird). Nests are usually low (Nickell's study of 629 regional nests showed an average of 3.5 feet above ground) but two were recorded at Rondeau at the abnormal heights of thirty-five and thirty-nine feet. The species is severely imposed on by the cowbird, with parasitism during some years as high as 56%. On the basis of 771 records in fifteen years, the average was 30%.

Magnolia Warbler   *Dendroica magnolia*

Common transient. Migrants normally arrive during first week of May (earliest: April 15, 1973), are most numerous around mid-month, and disappear in late May. There were a few early records of birds observed during the nesting season in the Port Huron Game Area, but the latest recent record was on June 5, 1971. Fall migrants reappear during last ten days of August (earliest banding record: August 9, 1964), and are recorded in the area throughout October (latest: October 31, 1951).

Cape May Warbler   *Dendroica tigrina*

Fairly common transient. Most spring birds reported from May 7 to 26 (earliest: April 30, 1951) in numbers varying greatly from year to year. Fall migrants usually reported from late August (earliest: August 12, 1972) through mid-October in smaller numbers than in spring. One late record: November 2, 1963.

Black-throated Blue Warbler   *Dendroica caerulescens*

Fairly common transient. Spring migration mainly concentrated in two middle weeks of May (earliest: April 29, 1964; latest: May 31, 1973). Except for two early records on August 8, 1954, and August 15, 1953, fall migration was reported from late August through October (latest: October 31, 1970).

Yellow-rumped (Myrtle) Warbler   *Dendroica coronata*

Common transient. Numerous in spring by mid-April; large numbers often reported. A straggler was present in Macomb County on June 13 and 20, 1970. Fall migrants reported as early as July 30, 1963, and three early August dates; most, however, are reported after mid-August. Migration is heaviest in October, gradually decreasing in November; consistently reported in winter in small numbers.

Black-throated Gray Warbler   *Dendroica nigrescens*

Accidental. One was picked up dead in Northville, Wayne County, on November 25, 1962, and given to Merriam (specimen UMMZ); second state record. Before this publication went to press, a second bird was observed at Greenfield Village, Wayne County, on April 29, 1975 (J. Fowler, Jr. and later the same day by J. Fowler, Sr.).

71

Townsend's Warbler
Dendroica townsendi

Accidental. A male was seen at Bradley's Marsh on May 15, 1966 (Kleiman). Another bird was observed at Pt. Pelee on May 10, 1972 (Chesterfield and others).

Black-throated Green Warbler
Dendroica virens

Common transient; rare summer resident. Spring migrants present through May (earliest: April 22, 1964), often in large numbers. Fall migrants regular by early September, numerous through early October, with scattered records through latest date, October 31, 1970.

Apparently breeds rarely and locally in four northernmost counties. Birds have been reported in summer in Highland Recreation Area and Port Huron Game Area through 1974, but without breeding evidence. Earlier records in 1953 and 1954 referred to adults feeding fledged young in Port Huron Game Area and extreme northwestern Macomb County.

Cerulean Warbler
Dendroica cerulia

Uncommon migrant and summer resident. Although spring migrants normally arrive during the first week of May, a few April birds were reported (earliest: April 19, 1959, a bird banded; and April 22, 1975, a sighting). Regularly reported from local areas through early July, with comparatively few records in the fall (latest: September 22, 1962, a bird banded).

Breeds regularly but locally in moderate numbers, mostly in mature deciduous woodlands. Definite records only for Oakland, Macomb, and St. Clair counties, but may be overlooked because it confines itself to uppermost forest canopy. Records refer to active but unexamined nests or to adults feeding fledged young (earliest: May 30, 1951, pair building a nest, Oakland County). Recent sight records in summer indicate breeding populations in Highland Recreation Area, Port Huron Game Area, and Rondeau.

Blackburnian Warbler
Dendroica fusca

Common transient. Spring migrants usually appear in early May; however, one was observed on April 6, 1947, the same date that two other species, Hooded Warbler (*Wilsonia citrina*) and Scarlet Tanager (*Piranga olivacea*), also appeared, a month early. Good numbers (up to thirty-five birds) recorded until last week in May. Recorded in June and July 1954 in Bruce Township, Macomb County, and consistently through 1974 in the Port Huron Game Area. Fall migration somewhat earlier than most warblers, near mid-August (earliest: August 5, 1964), and well under way soon thereafter, continuing through September; scattered records into October (latest: October 18, 1964).

Yellow-throated Warbler   *Dendroica dominica*

Rare visitant. Single birds reported from Pt. Pelee: May 19, 1946 (Zimmerman and others); May 2, 1962 (Botham); and May 20, 1969 (Baillie). One report from Rondeau on April 26, 1970 (Wilson). Formerly a rare resident in southern Michigan, but none reported from 1945 through 1974.

Chestnut-sided Warbler   *Dendroica pennsylvanica*

Fairly common transient; uncommon summer resident. Spring arrival usually in early May (earliest: April 30, 1950); peak migration from May 10 to 25 in numbers varying from year to year. Fall migrants evident by late August, with numbers increasing through mid-September, then decreasing through end of month. Two very late records: October 26, 1963, one banded; and November 23, 1974, one observed at Pt. Pelee.

Breeds casually and locally; status and distribution not well known, and no recent records. Four earlier records, three from Oakland County, and one from the Port Huron Game Area: June 17, 1951, adults feeding four young in nest; June 15, 1952, nest with two warbler eggs and two cowbird eggs; July 6, 1954, adults feeding young; June 23, 1956, adults building nest.

Bay-breasted Warbler   *Dendroica castanea*

Common transient, most numerous in fall. Spring migration does not usually begin until the second week in May (earliest: May 2, 1970), continuing throughout the month (latest: June 5, 1954). Fall migrants arrive near mid-August (earliest: August 10, 1964) and are regular throughout September and early October. Two late records: November 7, 1954, and November 8, 1962, both banded birds.

Blackpoll Warbler   *Dendroica striata*

Regular transient, more numerous in fall. Earliest spring arrivals: May 2 in 1953, 1969, and 1970. Migration heaviest after middle of month (latest: June 9, 1964). Generally reported in small numbers in spring; maximum of thirty-five birds at Pt. Pelee on May 25, 1974. Fall migrants usually appear in early September (earliest: August 18, 1960), numerous through October 10 with scattered reports through the end of the month (latest: November 3, 1961).

Pine Warbler   *Dendroica pinus*

Rare transient and summer resident. Earliest spring date: March 23, 1974. Six birds were reported that year from four stations, all in April, which is more than usual. Also scarce in fall; recorded most often from Pt. Pelee. Two unusual records, both in Detroit: a bird found dead on August 28, 1951, in an industrial section near downtown, the other a bird captured alive on the campus of Wayne State University on September 23, 1952 (later banded and released). Except for a bird on December 26, 1972, at Rondeau, the latest date was October 10, 1947.

Breeds in limited numbers and very locally in at least four northern-most survey counties. No nests found; all records refer to adults with fledged young from June 27 to July 19.

Kirtland's Warbler   *Dendroica kirtlandii*

Rare migrant. Four records. On May 10, 1953, a male was identified at Pt. Pelee by two groups (Miles first; then Sutton, Cook, and Parker). One was banded at the same place on May 10, 1959 (Wasserfall). An immature male was banded and photographed at the Cranbrook campus on September 24, 1965 (Nickell). An immature was identified near Davisburg, Oakland County, on August 7, 1973 (O'Reilly).

Prairie Warbler   *Dendroica discolor*

Rare transient and summer resident. Reported only in spring and early summer (earliest: May 2, 1964; no records after July 8); except for one report from Port Huron, all records were from the Canadian counties (Pt. Pelee, Bradley's Marsh, and Ipperwash Beach).

Although there are no recent records, it is known to have bred locally and in very small numbers in a narrow sandy area that skirts the southern shoreline of Lake Huron between Ipperwash Beach and Grand Bend in Bosanquet Township, Lambton County. Three breeding records from this area in 1954 in early July.

Palm Warbler   *Dendroica palmarum*

Common transient. Earliest arrival date: April 16, 1964; migrants numerous after May 1, particularly at Pt. Pelee, until latest date of May 24, 1952. Less numerous in fall; maximum of 175 birds on October 30, 1964. Migration extends from late August (earliest: August 23, 1952) through October with scattered November records and three later reports from Pt. Pelee on December 5, 1965; December 31, 1966; and January 3, 1966.

Ovenbird   *Seiurus aurocapillus*

Common transient and summer resident. Good numbers in spring by early May (earliest: April 19, 1947), more numerous than in the fall. Southward migration reported from late August until late October. Except for a bird banded on September 21, 1965, and recaptured on November 24, the latest date was October 25, 1953.

Breeds commonly in area, but not verified for all counties. Most reports refer to typical, well-concealed ground nests with four or five eggs; one atypical nest in Addison Township, Oakland County, had seven eggs, all of which hatched on June 14, 1952. Nesting may begin in mid-May (earliest: May 20, nest with five eggs), reaching peak in June and usually over by mid-July. Cowbird parasitism was 20.7% of total reports.

Northern Waterthrush   *Seiurus noveboracensis*

Uncommon transient and local summer resident. Spring arrival normally recorded in early May (earliest: April 20 and 21, 1964); recorded in summer from local areas. Fall migrants most numerous between August 20 and September 20, with scattered records (mostly banded birds) in October (latest: October 25, 1969).

Summer status and distribution of this and following species (*S. motacilla*) are confused because breeding ranges overlap. Between 1954 and 1960 a special investigation showed that the present species was breeding regularly in small numbers in extreme northwestern Macomb County and locally in northern Oakland County. There have been no actual nest records since then, but birds continue to be reported during nesting season. Early nest records were from boreal-type habitat of typical well-concealed nests in uprooted stumps or on the ground. Nesting dates were from June 5 to June 30, the latter of a nest with three eggs in Springfield Township, Oakland County.

Louisiana Waterthrush   *Seiurus motacilla*

Rare and local summer resident. Birds generally recorded in spring during middle two weeks of May (earliest: April 19, 1964, a bird banded). Most fall reports are from Pt. Pelee during last half of August (latest: September 23, 1949, and September 29, 1951).

Because of overlapping ranges and use of similar breeding habitat, the breeding status and distribution of this and the previous species (*S. noveboracensis*) are unclear. Recent banding records from the Port Huron Game Area show birds returning to same locality in early summer, evidently to nest; this is the most northern station in its Michigan range. In addition to nest records during the 1950s in Oakland, St. Clair, and Kent counties, a nest was found at Pt. Pelee in 1969 (earliest: May 27, 1950, nest with two warbler eggs and two cowbird eggs, Lake Orion). Most records refer to well-concealed nests. Before this publication went to press, a nest with one young was found at Highland Recreation Area on June 17, 1975.

Kentucky Warbler   *Oporornis formosus*

Rare visitant. Only four records from 1945 through 1957; since then, the species has been reported almost every year, regularly from

Pt. Pelee, but also from Kent, Wayne, Monroe, Oakland, and St. Clair counties (four birds banded). All records are in spring except two: a bird at Kensington Metropark on September 16, 1962, and two birds in the Port Huron Game Area on September 6, 1970.

Connecticut Warbler — *Oporornis agilis*

Regular but rare transient. Reported somewhat more often in spring than fall (from May 3 to early June); has evidently become more scarce in recent years. Fall migrants usually appear in late August (earliest: August 19, 1966), but very few reported; one October record on October 18, 1951.

Mourning Warbler — *Oporornis philadelphia*

Uncommon transient; rare local summer resident. Except for one early record (April 28, 1968), spring migrants were reported after May 10. Fall migration evident from late August to late September (latest: September 27, 1953) in very small numbers.

Apparently breeds locally in the four northernmost counties, but definite records only from Macomb and St. Clair counties; no recent nest records, but birds reported in similar local areas as previously. Early records (1953 and 1954) were of adults feeding fledged young on July 3 and July 10.

Common Yellowthroat — *Geothlypis trichas*

Common transient and summer resident. Spring migrants reach the area about the last week in April (earliest: April 24, 1972) and are often numerous in habitats such as Bradley's Marsh. Numbers decrease in fall through October; scattered reports in November and in winter (latest: February 9, 1973).

Breeds commonly, well-distributed, but not verified for all counties. Nesting generally begins in late May or early June, continues as late as mid-August, indicating occasional second broods. Nests are placed on or near the ground, well-concealed, and usually in moist situations. Earliest record: May 29, 1953, a nest with two eggs of host and two cowbird eggs. Six of twenty-seven reports showed cowbird parasitism.

Yellow-breasted Chat — *Icteria virens*

Uncommon summer resident. Regularly reported, most often in May (earliest: April 28, 1964), somewhat fewer in recent years. Present throughout summer, particularly in Essex and Monroe counties, but scarce after mid-July. Three December records in 1965 and 1966; one bird collected (UMMZ) on January 26, 1949, at Grosse Pointe, Wayne County.

Breeds locally in very small numbers, but probably now absent from previous stations in Bloomfield Township because of habitat destruction by suburban development. Earlier nesting data indicated nests confined largely to extensive tangles of dense shrubbery; earliest: June 12, 1949.

Hooded Warbler   *Wilsonia citrina*

Rare visitant and summer resident. One unusually early spring record: April 6, 1947; otherwise, earliest: April 21, 1974. Practically absent from 1951 to 1968, after which there have been regular reports from Pt. Pelee and other stations (six birds in spring of 1974). No late summer records and only two in fall (latest: September 23, 1951).

Apparently at extreme northern limit of breeding range in this latitude. Before 1951 singing males were recorded in summer in Kent (Thamesville and Rondeau), St. Clair (Port Huron Game Area), and Oakland (four townships) counties. From 1947 through 1951 a pair summered each year near Lake Orion, where Middleton and others produced four actual breeding records (earliest: May 27, 1951, newly completed nest which had two warbler eggs and two cowbird eggs by June 3). In 1972 and 1973 birds were present in mid-June at Highland Recreation Area: this appears to correspond to the increase in recent spring reports. Reports of birds in late May and early June (1968 and 1969) in suitable nesting habitat at Holly Recreation Area, Oakland County, and Stony Creek Metropark also seem significant.

Wilson's Warbler   *Wilsonia pusilla*

Uncommon transient. Arrival normally recorded after May 9 (earliest: April 28, 1964); four June reports (latest: June 6, 1971). Fall migration generally reported from late August (earliest: August 12, 1950) to mid-October, with two late October records (one of a banded bird) and one on November 10, 1972.

Canada Warbler   *Wilsonia canadensis*

Fairly common transient; previously rare and local summer resident. Like that of other late-arriving warblers, spring migration period is short, mainly during the last two weeks of May (earliest: May 7, 1950). From 1954 through 1959 the species was reported in summer from local areas in Macomb, Oakland, and St. Clair counties; no summer reports from 1959 until 1974 when two singing males were present in Highland Recreation Area. Fall migrants arrive early (August 7, 1949) and are regular by August 20; numbers decrease after mid-September, with scattered reports up to the latest date on October 9, 1954.

Breeding status and distribution unclear. In spite of reports of summering birds, nest records were obtained only from Bruce Township, Macomb County, from 1954 through 1959, evidently the southern-most Michigan breeding records. Six of nine reports refer to well-con-cealed nests on or near the ground from mid-June to mid-July (earliest: June 19, 1954, a nest with three eggs of host and one cowbird egg). Three reports refer to adults with young.

American Redstart *Setophaga ruticilla*

Common transient; fairly common summer resident. Arrival gener-ally reported in early May (earliest: May 1, 1950), becoming numerous through the month (several reports of 100 to 200 birds at Pt. Pelee and Rondeau). Fall migration heavy in September, gradually decreasing, with scattered records in late October and early November (latest: November 8, 1952).

Breeds regularly in fair numbers; no records from Wayne or Monroe counties. Locally common in mature, undisturbed woodlands, notably Rondeau. Occasional nests are completed in late May, but peak of nesting is reached in mid-June (earliest: May 22, 1954, a completed nest, Oakland County). Season continues throughout most of July, with interruptions and occasional second broods extending season to mid-August (latest: August 16, adult feeding three fledglings). Nests are usually found at moderate heights in small deciduous trees; four or five eggs are a normal clutch.

Family PLOCEIDE. Weaver Finches

House Sparrow *Passer domesticus*

Introduced species; permanent resident. Abundant, especially about farm buildings and residential areas.

Breeds abundantly, often monopolizing nest cavities at expense of more desirable species. Nest-building activities recorded in all seasons except coldest winter months; except for one record of young in nest on December 2, 1974, in Dearborn, Wayne County, eggs or young reported only for spring and summer. Two, and often three, broods are regularly raised in a season.

Family ICTERIDAE. Meadowlarks, Blackbirds, and Orioles

Bobolink *Dolichonyx oryzivorus*

Fairly common summer resident. Spring migration begins near mid-April (one unusually early record: March 31, 1967). Occasionally seen in large groups of 70 to 90 birds in late July and early August. Reported less frequently from mid-August to mid-September, scarce thereafter (latest: October 9, 1969). One report of 200 birds near Pt. Pelee on September 11, 1971.

78

Breeds commonly but somewhat locally; few actual nests found. Nests are placed on the ground in late May or early June (earliest: June 3, 1972, nest with eggs, Lambton County), well-concealed in high, heavy growth of clover (*Trifolium* sp.), alfalfa (*Medico* sp.), or similar plants. All reports for June or July (latest: July 25, 1954, female feeding fledgling, St. Clair County); no evidence of second broods.

Eastern Meadowlark   *Sturnella magna*

Common summer resident. Migration usually apparent in late February, but in small numbers in spring. Regular in summer, mainly in open country. Flocks (up to thirty birds) gather in August, with migration reported into November. Regularly reported in winter, occasionally in good numbers (thirty-nine birds in Kent County and sixteen in Essex County in winter of 1967).

Breeds commonly, well distributed. More than half of the records refer to nests with four or five eggs found in last half of May (earliest: April 28, 1953, nest with three eggs, Mt. Clemens). Scattered July and August dates evidently refer to second broods (latest: August 31, 1954, adult with flying young). Two instances of cowbird parasitism.

Western Meadowlark   *Sturnella neglecta*

Uncommon summer resident. A few reported each spring (March 6 to June 10) away from usual nesting areas. Status in fall and winter uncertain because of difficulty in identifying non-singing birds; however, a few singing birds were recorded in October (latest: October 5, 1947).

Five breeding records before 1959 (earliest: May 31, 1953, nest with five young): one from Oakland County, one from Essex County, and three from Macomb county. Since 1960 nesting has been reported only from Lambton County where a small colony has nested from 1967 through 1974.

Yellow-headed Blackbird   *Xanthocephalus xanthocephalus*

Rare visitant and summer resident. Three records before 1965 at Pte. Mouillee and Pt. Pelee; since then reported every year but one, mostly as single birds in large marshes at six stations, although most often at Bradley's Marsh; two records in December and two in January.

Two pairs reported nesting at Bradley's Marsh in the summer of 1966 (Sawyer and Dyer); four young fledged from one nest on June 25 and two young still in the second nest on June 30.

Red-winged Blackbird   *Agelaius phoeniceus*

Abundant summer resident. Spring migration gets under way with arrival of males about mid-February and is heavy by early March;

reported in large numbers. By August birds gather in flocks which increase in numbers throughout October (maximum of 30,000 on September 29, 1974, at Pt. Pelee) and diminish in November and December. Reported in some numbers in winter, particularly at Pt. Pelee and Rondeau (up to 3,000 in mixed flocks in late December).

Breeds abundantly throughout the area. Increase noted in recent years with a considerable number of nests in dry situations away from usual marshes; habitats include open fields, city parks, deciduous woods, suburban yards, and at least one in a hedgerow in a city neighborhood. Nesting usually begins by mid-May (earliest: April 26, 1968, nest with five eggs, Lambton County), peaks in late May and early June, is largely over by mid-July (latest: July 31, 1953, nest with two young). This species rarely tolerates interference by the cowbird; only fourteen cases of parasitism in more than 3,500 nests (one successful).

Orchard Oriole   *Icterus spurius*

Rare and local summer resident. Most numerous in May (earliest; April 18, 1964); reported in greatest numbers from Pt. Pelee and Bradley's Marsh, but no large numbers in recent years that compare with 129 birds at Pt. Pelee in May 1949. Some indication of flocking at Pt. Pelee in late July; very small numbers reported in August and September (latest: September 21, 1952).

Fourteen breeding records before 1955 from widely separated localities in Oakland, Macomb, Essex, and Kent counties (earliest: May 26, 1952, completed nest; latest: July 18, 1954, adult with one flying young). Very few nest records in recent years: one on June 10, 1965, from Kensington Metropark, and two later nests from Pt. Pelee. One instance of cowbird parasitism.

Northern (Baltimore) Oriole   *Icterus galbula*

Common summer resident. Spring migrants arrive in late April or early May (earliest: April 19, 1951). Following nesting season, usually after mid-July, good-sized flocks (80 to 125 birds) present at Pt. Pelee. Although migration is largely over by mid-September, there were several later records throughout October and early November. In 1967 a bird visited a Birmingham feeder throughout February and March; in the winter of 1972–73 one was seen at several feeders in Bloomfield Township from December through February.

Breeds commonly, well distributed. Since the disappearance of many elm (*Ulmus* sp.) trees, nests have been reported in a larger variety of deciduous trees than formerly. Nests sometimes completed by mid-May (earliest: May 12, nest under construction) but usually late May or early June (latest: July 20, 1953, active nest, Oakland County). No evidence of more than one brood.

Rusty Blackbird *Euphagus carolinus*

Common transient. Spring migrants evident from mid-March through late May and early June (latest: June 7, 1954), occasionally in flocks of up to 1,000 birds. Main fall migration begins in early October, with scattered earlier records (earliest: August 28, 1953), and continues throughout November. Several winter reports, including 30 birds at Bradley's Marsh on January 23, 1960.

Brewer's Blackbird *Euphagus cyanocephalus*

Rare migrant and summer resident. Eight reports of one or two birds: three from Pt. Pelee, two each from Kent and Oakland counties, and one from Macomb County. These birds reported only in spring and fall.

In addition to the above, two pairs nested in summer of 1966 near Pontiac Lake (young banded; Hirt and Piotter). A group of six birds, possibly a family, sighted at a sod farm in Oakland County on July 6, 1974 (E. and H. Cox).

Common Grackle *Quiscalus quiscula*

Abundant summer resident. Common in spring by mid-March, abundant soon thereafter, remaining so throughout summer and fall. Large flocks of several thousand birds reported in fall, with a considerable increase in numbers in recent years. Migration largely over by November. Consistently reported in winter, particularly numerous in mixed flocks at Rondeau and Pt. Pelee.

Breeds abundantly, widely distributed. Nesting normally begins in early April (reports of several nests under construction by April 2); average clutches of four or five eggs often completed by third week. Nesting season largely over by mid-June; scattered records in early July (latest: July 15, 1953, adult with four young) probably represent renestings after first failures. Nests frequently placed in conifers (sometimes in a semicolonial situation) at varying heights and occasionally in wet situations shared by Red-winged Blackbirds (*Agelaius phoeniceus*).

Brown-headed Cowbird *Molothrus ater*

Abundant summer resident. Spring migrants common by end of March, abundant soon thereafter. By early August large flocks are reported, increasing through October (up to several thousand birds). Regularly reported in winter, but found in large numbers only in the marshes of Canadian counties (2,000 at Rondeau on December 28, 1970).

Breeding populations fluctuate from year to year; generally more numerous in recent years. Survey records show forty-seven species of small altricial birds imposed upon by this social parasitic species. Incidence rates were highest for the Red-eyed Vireo (*Vireo olivaceus*), followed by the Song Sparrow (*Melospiza melodia*) and the Yellow Warbler (*Dendroica petechia*). In cases of less common hosts at the fringes of their breeding range, heavy parasitism may be a limiting factor, possibly so with the Yellow-breasted Chat (*Icteria virens*) and the Prairie Warbler (*Dendroica discolor*).

Family THRAUPIDAE. Tanagers

Western Tanager   *Piranga ludoviciana*

Accidental. A male was seen at Kensington Metropark on April 27, 1965 (Curtis). A second male was observed at Bradley's Marsh on May 10, 1969 (Pesold).

Scarlet Tanager   *Piranga olivacea*

Common summer resident. Arrival generally reported in early May; two very early records: April 6, 1947, and April 11, 1974. A few spring records of twenty to fifty birds at migration points; less numerous in fall. Reported throughout September with three October records and two in November (latest: November 25, 1962).

Breeds regularly in moderate numbers; may be fairly common locally in mature deciduous woodlands such as Rondeau. Nests sometimes begun in late May (earliest: May 9, 1953, a female at a completed nest), but majority of reports were in June and early July with three or four eggs or young. A few later records indicate occasional second broods may be raised (latest: August 2, 1953, a male feeding a fledgling cowbird).

Summer Tanager   *Piranga rubra*

Rare visitant. Seven reports before 1964; since then it has been reported regularly each year, except 1967, at Pt. Pelee (five different birds in May 1972). Reported also from Rondeau, Grand Lawn Cemetery (Wayne County), Belle Isle, and Stony Creek Metropark.

Family FRINGILLIDAE. Grosbeaks, Finches, Sparrows, and Buntings

Cardinal   *Cardinalis cardinalis*

Common permanent resident. Regularly reported in all seasons from both urban and rural areas. Sometimes found in flocks of 20 to 55 birds during winter in areas of good food supply. Good numbers on Christmas Counts with a maximum of 496 in the Detroit Audubon Society count of December 1970.

Breeds commonly, widely distributed. This species has the longest nesting period of any area species except the Mourning Dove (*Aenaidura macroura*) (earliest: April 6, 1969; latest: October 8, 1974, male feeding young, Detroit); both raise more than one brood. Nests are often concealed in shrubbery at low elevations; about 12% showed cowbird parasitism.

Rose-breasted Grosbeak   *Pheucticus ludovicianus*

Common summer resident. Spring arrival generally reported in late April or first few days of May (earliest: April 19, 1948). Reported infrequently after the nesting season except for some migration evidenced in the first three weeks of September; two October records and a late bird on November 12, 1972.

Breeds regularly but locally; most reports from Oakland and St. Clair counties. Nesting begins about mid-May (earliest: May 19, 1951, a female incubating) with eggs reported from third week of May well into June. Two July reports (latest: July 22, 1954) indicate that normally only one brood is raised. Four reports of incubating males singing on the nest. Four instances of cowbird parasitism.

Blue Grosbeak   *Guiraca caerulea*

Accidental. Three records, all at Pt. Pelee: May 15, 1964 (Baillie and O'Grady); May 31, 1967 (Mara); May 7 to 20, 1971 (Greenhouse and others).

Indigo Bunting   *Passerina cyanea*

Common summer resident. Arrival normally reported in early May (earliest: April 27, 1957) in small numbers. Regularly reported through mid-August, less frequently in September; four October records (latest: October 16, 1971).

Breeds regularly, well distributed. Nesting occasionally begins in late May (earliest: May 24, 1953, a completed nest in Ray Township, Macomb County), but majority of nests with eggs are reported after mid-June. Reports for late July and early August probably represent renestings (latest: August 19, 1951, nest with three eggs, Warren Township, Macomb County); second broods may sometimes be raised.

Painted Bunting   *Passerina ciris*

Accidental. A male visited a feeder in Port Huron on May 2, 1973 (photographed by Lamb).

Dickcissel   *Spiza americana*

Rare, irregular transient and summer resident. Reported somewhat more regularly after 1966, most often from Pt. Pelee, where two pairs were present in the summer of 1967, and from Monroe County, where several pairs made up a small colony in summer of 1972 and 1973. No nesting evidence.

Evening Grosbeak   *Hesperiphona vespertina*

Irregular winter visitant. Reported in varying numbers practically every year. Heavy invasions reported in winters of 1949–50, 1951–52, 1961–62, and 1968–69. Earliest arrival: September 15, 1974; in winters of large invasions birds remained well into May (latest: May 25, 1969).

Purple Finch   *Carpodacus purpureus*

Fairly common winter visitant; local and rare summer resident. Fall arrival usually reported about mid-September, occasionally in good-sized flocks (up to 340 birds at Kettle Point from October 13 to 18, 1974). Regularly reported throughout winter, gradually disappearing in May.

Four breeding records, the first two in Oakland County in 1954 and 1955. Two recent records in 1964: May 23, nest with four eggs in Clyde Township, St. Clair County; July 2, adult feeding fledged young in Bosanquet Township, Lambton County. Stanton observed a pair at his evergreen plantation on Grosse Ile through the summers of 1965 and 1966, but no nest was found.

Pine Grosbeak   *Pinicola enucleator*

Irregular winter visitant. Reported in small numbers in less than half of the fall-winter periods. Numerous only during an invasion of several hundred birds between November 10, 1951, and March 2, 1952, mostly in Oakland County. Generally recorded from November into March (latest: March 23, 1958).

Hoary Redpoll   *Acanthis hornemanni*

Accidental. Four birds photographed or banded when they appeared during invasions of Common Redpolls (*A. flammea*). In 1968 two birds were found at Sarnia: one identified on October 23 (Rupert), and one photographed on November 23 (John). Two birds were banded in February 1972, one at St. Clair Shores, Macomb County (Ryff and Radcliffe) and another at Marysville, St. Clair County (Douville and Lamb).

Common Redpoll   *Acanthis flammea*

Irregular winter visitant. Reported in greatly varying numbers; more numerous in invasions after 1965. In the fall and winter of 1968–69, a total of more than 3,000 birds was reported; even more abundant in the winter of 1971–72 when birds appeared at feeders throughout the area and large numbers (690 on the Detroit Audubon Society Christmas Count) were found in weedy fields. Reported from earliest date of October 24, 1954 to April 15, 1970.

Pine Siskin   *Spinus pinus*

Irregular winter visitor; rare summer resident. Recorded most winters in generally small numbers; large invasions in five winters, notably in the successive winters of 1971–72 and 1972–73. Following each of these, birds remained to nest: June 13, 1972, adult feeding two fledged young, Detroit (Cox) and April 27, 1973, one young fledged from nest, Birmingham, Oakland County (Greenhouse). In addition, in late March 1973 five birds were seen with nesting material in the same Detroit area as in 1972. A fledged young, barely able to fly, was banded in Bloomfield Township on June 25, 1963 (Bailey). Eight birds were seen at Rondeau on August 10, 1969, an unusual date.

American Goldfinch   *Spinus tristis*

Common permanent resident. Most numerous in fall (1,000 birds at Pt. Pelee on October 5, 1974); large numbers (up to 2,000) counted during fall hawk watch at Holiday Beach as they crossed the Detroit River. Good numbers also in winter (782 on 1968 Detroit Audubon Society Christmas Count).

Breeds commonly in all survey counties. Nesting is later than that of any other species, rarely before first week of July (earliest: June 29, 1952, female at nest with two cowbird eggs); most nests reported between first and third weeks of August, indicating height of season. Active nests in first half of September probably represent second broods or renestings after interruptions (latest: September 21, 1973, nest with young; September 24, 1970, nest with four well-grown young). Five eggs constitute a normal clutch, although nests were found with four and six eggs and one with seven.

Red Crossbill   *Loxia curvirostra*

Irregular visitant. Reported most often in fall and winter but found in all seasons. Numerous in two periods: spring of 1951 (maximum of sixty birds) and winter of 1972–73. Several June reports, three in July (July 12, 1969; July 14, 1973; July 30, 1972); all summer reports are from Rondeau or various stations in Lambton County.

White-winged Crossbill   *Loxia leucoptera*

Irregular visitant. Less numerous than Red Crossbill (*L. curvirostra*);

reported in seven different years, usually in small numbers. Light invasions in winter of 1954, fall of 1969, and fall and winter of 1971–72 (maximum of 132 birds at Ipperwash Beach). Reported twice in spring (20 on March 25, 1954, Kensington Metropark, and one on May 21, 1974, Mt. Clemens) and once in summer (June 5, 1974, a female in the Port Huron Game Area).

Rufous-sided Towhee   *Pipilo erythrophthalmus*

Common summer resident. Spring migration evident about mid-March, heavy by early April. No increase in numbers in fall, but a gradual decrease after mid-October. Regularly reported throughout winter in small numbers.

Breeds commonly. Nesting usually begins in mid-May (earliest: April 27, 1955, pair building nest) and extends well in August (latest: September 13, 1954, female with three young). First nests are usually on or near the ground; second nests are often placed higher in shrubs, but at low elevations. One nest, however, was found at an estimated height of fifteen feet above the ground in an oak tree (*Quercus* sp.) at Pontiac Lake. About 25% of the nests reported were parasitized by cowbirds.

Lark Bunting   *Calamospiza melanocorys*

Vagrant. Two records: a male found in the unlikely location of a parking lot at the Fisher Building in Detroit (J. and J. Bartell); the second bird was observed at Pt. Pelee on May 17 and 18, 1974, and photographed (Rupert and others).

Savannah Sparrow   *Passerculus sandwichensis*

Common summer resident. Migrants usually arrive in early April (earliest: March 27, 1947), common by the last week. Regularly reported throughout summer with numbers decreasing in August; infrequently reported through November. Five winter records.

Breeds regularly; somewhat reduced in recent years. Some nests with eggs reported by mid-May (earliest: May 5, 1955, nest with five eggs of host and one cowbird egg), but records indicate peak of season is the first half of June. Scattered reports until late July suggest second broods (latest: July 25, 1954, adult feeding two fledglings). Most nests were found in meadows, fields, or similar dry situations.

Grasshopper Sparrow   *Ammodramus savannarum*

Uncommon summer resident. Arrival usually reported in late April (earliest: April 24, 1954), then in small numbers throughout spring and summer. Few reports after mid-August (latest: October 10, 1954).

Breeds in small numbers, locally, with distribution not clearly defined. Seven actual nests, all but one (nest with eggs at Pt. Pelee on June 16, 1969) before 1958. Dates range from May 28 (nest with five eggs) to July 22 (pair with newly fledged young). Somewhat more numerous during nesting season since 1970, particularly at Stony Creek Metropark and locally in Lambton County.

Henslow's Sparrow   *Ammodramus henslowii*

Uncommon summer resident. Usually reported in late April or early May (earliest: April 12, 1969), regular through July. One recent spring record of an unusually large number (100 birds) at Stony Creek Metropark on April 30, 1974. Few reports after mid-August; one very late bird banded on October 18, 1953.

Breeds irregularly and locally in varying numbers. Generally scarce in nesting season in recent years except for local "colony" at Stony Creek Metropark, where the population appears fairly stable. Six breeding records before 1959 from Oakland and Macomb counties between June 3 (nest with five eggs) and July 9 (adults with two young).

Le Conte's Sparrow   *Ammospiza lecontii*

Rare transient. Reported only from Pt. Pelee. Eleven birds recorded in spring from April 20 to May 18; two birds in fall, one on October 16, 1965 (Kleiman and Postupalsky), another on October 27, 1973 (Maley and Overman).

Sharp-tailed Sparrow   *Ammospiza caudacuta*

A bird of this species was observed at Pt. Pelee on May 16 and 25, 1974 (Rupert).

Vesper Sparrow   *Pooecetes gramineus*

Common summer resident. Arrival usually reported in late March, common by second week in April, although in small numbers. Regularly reported throughout summer and fall until early November; scarce thereafter, but a few birds (one to five) reported in most winters.

Breeds commonly, with a preference for dry, upland fields or roadsides. Nesting usually begins around mid-May (earliest: April 28, nest with four eggs), peaking in June; may be extended into July by interruptions or second broods (latest: July 25, 1954, an adult feeding a full-grown young).

Lark Sparrow   *Chondestes grammacus*

Rare migrant. Eight reports between April 11 and May 10; four from Pt. Pelee, two from Rondeau, one from Harsens Island, and one (two birds) from Bald Mountain Recreation Area, Oakland County.

Bachman's Sparrow   *Aimophila aestivalis*

Accidental. A singing male was found in Dearborn, Wayne County, on May 8, 1946 (Miller). It remained in the area until May 13 when it was collected (O'Reilly; UMMZ).

Cassin's Sparrow   *Aimophila cassinii*

Accidental. One report of a bird at Pt. Pelee on May 13, 1967 (photographed by Critch; seen also by Long and many others).

Dark-eyed (Slate-colored) Junco   *Junco hyemalis*

Abundant transient and winter visitor. Arrival generally reported around mid-September (earliest: September 3, 1960, and September 5, 1972), numerous soon thereafter. Generally abundant throughout winter (with numbers varying yearly) and spring (most numerous in April). Scattered reports in May; except for a singing male on July 5, 1953, at Rondeau, the latest date was May 30, 1952.

Tree Sparrow   *Spizella arborea*

Abundant transient and winter visitor. Fall migrants arrive in late September or early October (earliest: September 25, 1952), common by end of October. Regularly reported throughout winter in flocks up to 500 birds. Spring migration evident in March and April, after which numbers diminish rapidly (latest: May 15, 1965).

Chipping Sparrow   *Spizella passerina*

Common summer resident. Spring migrants generally reported about the first of April, common by late April. Most have left the area in fall by early November, although a few recorded in winter in recent years.

Breeds commonly throughout the area, somewhat reduced in recent years. Nesting occasionally begins by mid-May (earliest: May 11, 1972, nest under construction), but more common later in the month; continues well into August (latest: August 27, 1954). About 20% of the 135 nests reported showed cowbird parasitism.

Clay-colored Sparrow   *Spizella pallida*

Rare transient and summer resident. Fifteen reports before 1968, all from Pt. Pelee except one from Ipperwash Beach and one from Port Huron Game Area. Since then one or two birds have been reported between May 2 to 24 each year except 1973, five times from Pt. Pelee and once each from Rondeau, Sarnia, and Mt. Clemens.

One breeding record. A nest with three eggs found in Kenockee Township, St. Clair County, on July 5, 1962 (Lamb), about ten inches up in a small planted Jack Pine (*Pinus banksiana*). The eggs hatched on July 10, and the young were banded on July 15 by Lamb who had previously mist-netted and banded the adults. This is evidently the most southerly nesting record for the species which had not previously been known to nest south of Ogemaw and Roscommon counties (Zimmerman and Van Tyne, 1959). Since 1962 birds have been banded in the same general area of St. Clair County from May to mid-June, but no nests have been found.

Field Sparrow   *Spizella pusilla*

Common summer resident. First spring migrants usually reported in mid-March, common after first week in April. Sometimes reported in large numbers (100 to 300 birds) at Pt. Pelee. Regular through summer and fall, becoming scarce in November. Scattered winter reports, especially at feeders; 34 birds reported on the Kent County Christmas Count in late December 1971.

Breeds commonly, well distributed, usually in dry grassy areas such as abandoned fields or pastures. Nesting begins by mid-May (earliest: May 8, 1952, two nests with four eggs each), peaking about mid-June. First nests are almost always placed on the ground, but as foliage develops later nests are often concealed in shrubs three or four feet above the ground (latest: August 25, 1953, a nest with two young).

Harris' Sparrow   *Zonotrichia querula*

Accidental. Six reports of single birds at Pt. Pelee: four in May, one on March 28, 1968, and one of a bird which remained from January through March 1966. Two birds were present at Rondeau on May 10 and 11, 1970 (photographed by Simpson and Rupert).

White-crowned Sparrow   *Zonotrichia leucophrys*

Common transient. Except for a straggler banded in Bloomfield Township on July 4, 1964, the latest spring migrant was noted on June 4, 1970. Fall birds normally appear in late September (earliest: September 17, 1951) and are common until late October. Scattered reports in winter indicate an increase in recent years (up to 20 birds reported in winter of 1971–72). One extremely large concentration was present at Pt. Pelee on May 10, 1952, when birds of many species arrived in extraordinary numbers with delayed frontal passage; 12,000 birds of this species were estimated to be present and 20,000 of the following species (*Z. albicollis*).

White-throated Sparrow   *Zonotrichia albicollis*

Abundant transient. Migrants arrive about mid-April, numerous until late May (latest: May 29, 1964). In 1954 a singing male was observed several times in Grant Township, St. Clair County, from July 11 to August 2; in 1971 single birds were reported in Rochester, Oakland County, and Erie Marsh in July. Fall migration begins about mid-September (earliest: September 3, 1950; September 4, 1972), is heavy throughout October, and decreases in November. Regular in small numbers throughout winter.

Fox Sparrow   *Passerella iliaca*

Fairly common transient. Arrival generally recorded in late March (earliest: March 14, 1964); migration obvious until mid-May (latest: May 15, 1951). Numbers vary in spring, but are reduced in recent years compared with totals of 100 to 200 reported in 1950 and 1953. Fall migration extends from late September (earliest: September 19, 1953) through November; eight scattered winter records.

Lincoln's Sparrow   *Melospiza lincolnii*

Uncommon transient. Reported in spring from May 1 to 31, usually in small numbers. Banding records have shown this retiring species to be more numerous in fall migration (earliest: September 7, 1948) than previously known. In the fall of 1960 banding nets set in a weedy, previously fertilized, field now grown to rough pigweed (*Amaranthus retroflexus*) produced a total of thirty-nine birds; in 1962, fifty-one birds. Scattered November records and one at Pt. Pelee on December 14, 1966

Swamp Sparrow   *Melospiza georgiana*

Common transient and summer resident. Migration begins in early April, heavy from late April to mid-May; sometimes fairly numerous (25 to 100 birds) at Pt. Pelee, Bradley's Marsh, and Harsens Island. Common in fall through early November, fewer thereafter, although reported throughout winter (up to 45 birds in the larger marshes).

Breeds regularly, but comparatively few nests located. Nesting begins by mid-May (earliest: May 1, 1954, nest with four eggs) and reaches peak in June; may extend to mid-July with interruptions or occasional second broods (latest: July 14, 1954, nest with three young). Well-concealed nests are invariably placed in swampy or wet situations.

Song Sparrow   *Melospiza melodia*

Abundant transient and summer resident; fairly common winter resident. Reported in good numbers (up to 200 birds) in spring from

90

early March through May. Remains numerous in summer and fall, decreasing in November and December; regularly reported throughout winter, with concentrations at Erie Marsh, Pt. Pelee, and Rondeau.

Breeds abundantly, widely distributed, nests sometimes begun in April (earliest: April 24, 1952, nest with six eggs), but more often about second week in May; height of season from mid-May to mid-June. Since the species frequently raises two broods, the nesting season extends into August (latest: August 31, 1973, nest with three young). Of the approximately 260 recorded nests, about 30% showed cowbird parasitism.

Lapland Longspur   *Calcarius lapponicus*

Uncommon transient and winter visitant. Reported most often in open fields with Snow Buntings (*Plectrophenax nivalis*) and Horned Larks (*Eremophila alpestris*). Arrival usually reported in late September (earliest: September 25, 1954); most numerous in October and November. Latest spring record: May 15, 1964. Five reports of good numbers (25 to 100 birds).

Snow Bunting   *Plectrophenax nivalis*

Common winter visitant. Fall arrival generally reported in late October (earliest: October 3, 1953); most have left by mid-March (two April records; latest: April 13, 1974). Often found in large flocks in open fields and along roadsides, particularly in Lambton and Kent counties; two reports of more than 1,000 birds, and one flock on January 1, 1970, was estimated at 10,000 birds

NAMES OF OBSERVERS CITED IN TEXT

Karl D. Bailey
James L. Baillie
Paul Barker
Judy Bartell
Joseph Bartell
Charles T. Black
Wilfred Botham
D. Broughton
Bertha F. Carter
Norman Chesterfield
Frank Cook
Ellie Cox
W. V. Critch
L. Curtis
Bertha Daubendiek
Clayton Douville
Douglas Dow
M. I. Dyer
Richard Eldon
William Fisher
James A. Fowler, Jr.
James A. Fowler, Sr.
Rowley Frith
Victor Goodwill
Lester Gray
Jeffrey A. Greenhouse
William W. H. Gunn
Paul Hamel
Barbara L. Hirt
George Holland
Helen M. Horton
Joseph R. Jehl
Roy John
Paul J. G. Kidd
Edna Kiefer
Joseph P. Kleiman
Dorothy Lamb
Warren A. Lamb
Thomas H. Langlois
Lawrence R. Lenz
J. David Ligon
C. Long
Alfred Maley

Robert E. Mara
Malcolm McDonald
Robin D. Merriam
Douglas S. Middleton
Vaden Miles
Alice D. Miller
Brian Morin
Walter P. Nickell
Thomas H. Notebaert
W. O'Grady
Ralph A. O'Reilly, Jr.
Karl Overman
J. Parker
William Pesold
Harold Peters
Benedict C. Pinkowski
Joyce Piotter
Sergej Postupalsky
Paul Pratt
Rebecca Radcliffe
Norman Randall
Keith Reynolds
Mildred Reynolds
Alfred Rider
Dennis Rupert
Alan J. Ryff
M. Sawyer
William Schlageter
Robert Simpson
Ernest N. Stanton
George S. Stirrett
William Sutton
Sally Thompson
Harrison B. Tordoff
Richard Ussher
Allen E. Valentine
Laurel Van Camp
Norman Vogel
William Wasserfall
LaRue Wells
James W. Wilson
William Wyett
Dale A. Zimmerman

LITERATURE CITED

American Ornithologists' Union
    1957   Check-list of North American birds.
           Lancaster, Pennsylvania.

American Ornithologists' Union
    1973   Thirty-second supplement to the American Ornithologists'
           Union check-list of North American birds.
           Auk 90: 411–419

Kelley, Alice H., Douglas S. Middleton, Walter P. Nickell
    1963   Birds of the Detroit-Windsor area, a ten-year
           survey.
           Bloomfield Hills, Michigan: Cranbrook Institute
           of Science.

Zimmerman, Dale A. and Josselyn Van Tyne
    1959   A distributional check-list of the birds of
           Michigan.
           Occasional Papers number 608.
           Ann Arbor, Michigan: University of Michigan
           Museum of Zoology.

INDEX OF SPECIES

94